NATURE
HIKES

NATURE HIKES

NEAR-TORONTO TRAILS AND ADVENTURES

JANET EAGLESON

PHOTOGRAPHS BY ROSEMARY G. HASNER

The BOSTON
MILLS PRESS

Canadian Cataloguing in Publication Data

Eagleson, Janet, 1968–
Nature hikes: Near-Toronto trails and adventures

ISBN 1-55046-324-1

1. Trails – Ontario – Toronto Region – Guidebooks. 2. Natural resources
conservation areas – Ontario – Toronto – Guidebooks. 3. Hiking – Ontario – Toronto
Region – Guidebooks. 4. Toronto Region (Ont.) – Guidebooks. I. Title.

FC3097.18.E23 2000   917.13'541044   C00-930609-9
F1059.5.T683 2000

Published in 2000 by
BOSTON MILLS PRESS
132 Main Street
Erin, Ontario N0B 1T0
Tel 519-833-2407
Fax 519-833-2195
e-mail books@bostonmillspress.com
www.bostonmillspress.com

An affiliate of
STODDART PUBLISHING CO. LIMITED
34 Lesmill Road
Toronto, Ontario, Canada
M3B 2T6
Tel 416-445-3333
Fax 416-445-5967
e-mail gdsinc@genpub.com

Distributed in Canada by
GENERAL DISTRIBUTION SERVICES LIMITED
325 Humber College Boulevard
Toronto, Canada M9W 7C3
Orders 1-800-387-0141 Ontario & Quebec
Orders 1-800-387-0172
NW Ontario & other provinces
e-mail cservice@genpub.com

Distributed in the United States by
GENERAL DISTRIBUTION SERVICES INC.
PMB 128, 4500 Witmer Industrial Estates
Niagara Falls, New York 14305-1386
Toll-free 1-800-805-1083
Toll-free fax 1-800-481-6207
e-mail gdsinc@genpub.com
www.genpub.com

Design by Gillian Stead
Maps and illustrations by Rosemary Hasner
Printed in Canada by Friesen Printers

OVERLEAF:
Surveying the scene from the edge of the shinglebar.

*We acknowledge for their financial support of our publishing
program the Canada Council, the Ontario Arts Council, and
the Government of Canada through the Book Publishing
Industry Development Program (BPIDP).*

Acknowledgements

T his book would not have been possible without the hard work of a number of dedicated professionals and volunteers in the conservation field. These people work tirelessly to ensure that our local natural environment is protected from the rapid growth of urbanization that surrounds us all.

The Conservation Foundation acknowledges the stewardship of staff, volunteers, donors and municipal governments who support the important work of the Central Lake Ontario, Credit Valley, Lake Simcoe Region, Nottawasaga Valley and The Toronto and Region Conservation Authorities.

A young buck appears out of nowhere.

Contents

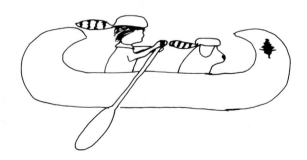

Foreword

**"The future of the planet will be decided in the next 25 years...
one living thing at a time."**

I t is estimated that in only the last 50 years of the last century,
humans have consumed more natural resources and produced
more waste and pollution than in the history of humankind.
The global repercussions of our behaviours are daunting:

- one species becomes extinct on the planet every single day
- forests and green spaces are disappearing at alarming rates
- toxins in our soil are leaching into the food chain
- the rate of respiratory disease is escalating
- water — the lifeblood of all living things — is no longer safe to
  drink in many parts of the world

The list goes on.

At no point in our history has the urgency for environmental and
conservation leadership been greater. And nowhere is the challenge
more important than in the urban and urbanizing regions in South
Central Ontario. The Conservation Foundation, along with its
partner Conservation Authorities, believes that concern for the global
environment begins at home, in the places where we live and play.
In the last 39 years, the Conservation Foundation has raised and
invested more than $13 million in practical solutions to protect,
regenerate and restore the environment in and around Canada's
largest city. Through the power of local partnerships and action, the
Conservation Foundation offers donors local solutions to their global
environmental concerns.

Their prescription for environmental health is simple and practical:

1. protect, monitor and restore regional biodiversity,
2. restore what is degraded,
3. educate the public on better environmental practices,
4. plan for a sustainable urban and near-urban region,
5. use the best science available, and
6. take personal responsibility to improve their own backyard.

With this powerful vision, the Conservation Foundation and its Conservation Authority partners are helping to improve local environmental health today and shape a world our grandchildren will enjoy tomorrow.

You can help! Join the Conservation Foundation as a supporter and do your part for the local — and global — environments!

For more information on the Conservation Foundation and to contribute to their local environmental programs, call (416) 667-6296.

Introduction

Close your eyes and imagine your favourite moment in the great outdoors. Perhaps it's that instant, just after the rain stops, when the pine forest smells so green. Maybe it's the thrill of seeing your first black and white warbler creeping around a branch, just an arm's length away. It could be the rush of adrenaline that surges through your body as you approach the edge of a sheer rock face. Or maybe, very simply, it's that moment of relief when you realize that the tiny hiker beside you actually enjoys nature more than that television show you hate so much.

Welcome to *Nature Hikes: Near-Toronto Trails and Adventures*, a book that celebrates the natural world and recognizes that nature touches each of us in very different ways. As you thumb through the pages that follow, you will be introduced to the many treasures of natural resources and wildlife habitats that you can discover close to your own home. These areas have been protected by your local Conservation Authority, which works diligently to preserve the quality and health of your regional environment.

CONSERVATION JOURNEYS

Nature Hikes supports Conservation Journeys, a membership program that believes the environment we should be most concerned about is the one in our own backyard. The Conservation Journeys memberships provide year-round unlimited access to some 22,680 hectares of truly extraordinary near-urban wilderness lands. These lands have been preserved and protected by the Conservation Foundation and five Conservation Authorities in South Central Ontario: Central Lake Ontario Conservation, Credit Valley Conservation, Lake Simcoe Region Conservation, Nottawasaga Valley Conservation, and Toronto and Region Conservation.

USING THIS BOOK

For your convenience, this book is organized into geographic sections — east, west, north, south and central. Each Conservation Area or park includes a summary of critical site information, an at-a-glance activity list, a map of the trails, and a first-person interpretive account of everything from flora and fauna to geology and history. The stories you will soon read are factually accurate but their tone is definitely casual — if you're looking for a traditional field guide, this book is not for you. The stories reflect the many different experiences I stumbled upon (or fell over) during my outdoor adventures.

RESPECT FOR NATURE

As you make your way along the pathways described in Nature Hikes, you will be struck by both the majesty and the delicacy of our natural world. With this in mind, I hope that you continue to develop a respectful relationship with nature. Always keep your dogs on a leash. Please stay on the designated trails to avoid damage to sensitive vegetation. View wildlife quietly from a distance. Baby birds and animals may be adorable, but please do not approach nests or dens. The stress of your approach is likely to drive the adult bird or animal away, causing them to leave their eggs or their young vulnerable to predators or extreme weather. If you see a young bird or baby animal that seems either to have fallen from its nest or to have been abandoned, do not touch it. Most of these seemingly helpless creatures are actually being cared for by their parents and are more likely to survive in their parents' care than yours. It is also good to remember that while sunscreen and insect repellent are essential for humans, they leave oils on your fingers that can cause considerable harm to wildflowers, insects, frogs, salamanders and just about every species of flora and fauna imaginable. Please look without touching, take out everything you bring into an area and leave only with photographs.

Nature provides different meanings and different inspirations to everyone. The beautiful parks in Nature Hikes: Near-Toronto Trails and Adventures have captured my imagination and my soul... I hope they capture yours, too.

E A S T

Take refuge beneath the dramatic canopy of trees.

Purple Woods Conservation Area

Birdwatching

Photography

Maple Syrup

Dogs on Leash Allowed

HIGHLIGHTS   The view stretches all the way to the CN Tower. Located on the beautiful Oak Ridges Moraine.

DIFFICULTY   Novice

TRAIL   Length: 1 km
MARKERS   n/a
SURFACE   Screened gravel and forest path

TYPE   Linear

FACILITIES   Parking, washrooms
only during maple syrup program.

OPEN   Year-round access
(maintained from March through Thanksgiving).

OWNED AND OPERATED BY
Central Lake Ontario Conservation Authority

DIRECTIONS   Exit Highway 401 at Simcoe Street in Oshawa and travel north on Simcoe to Coates Road (10th Concession). Turn right onto Coates Road, and you'll see the Purple Woods parking lot immediately on the right hand side.

One day when I was a young child, my father took my brother and me into the woods on our farm to show us our family's signpost. I think I was about seven at the time and I wasn't exactly sure why there would be a sign in the middle of the bush, but I happily went along because it was an adventure with my dad. He took us to an old American beech tree that was way wider than I was. There, carved into the bark, were the initials of my grandfather and his children, including my dad. My brother and I touched the raised bark in wide-eyed wonder, and then dad took out his jackknife and proudly wrote our initials there, too. The first time I visited Purple Woods, it took me a few minutes to realize why the place had such a familiar feel — the "purple" woods were actually American beech trees.

Poetic musings on an American beech.

The trunk of an American beech tree looks a bit like an elephant leg. The bark is smooth and grey, and seems more like skin than actual bark. Like skin, beech bark is thin and scars permanently when it's injured or cut. For centuries, these trees have been used to proclaim never-ending love, to record enduring family histories or just to make a commentary on the day. Unfortunately, bark wounds allow wood-rotting fungus to penetrate the tree's skin, and a single cut may cause the tree to die a slow and painful death. Sadly, the practice of poetic carving continues today.

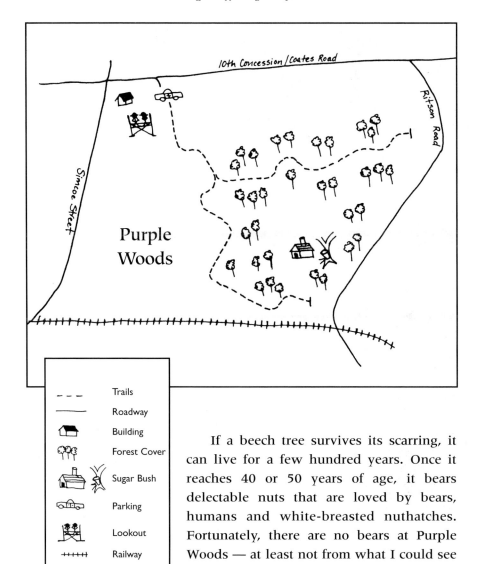

10th Concession/Coates Road

Ritson Road

Simcoe Street

Purple
Woods

Trails
Roadway
Building
Forest Cover
Sugar Bush
Parking
Lookout
Railway

If a beech tree survives its scarring, it can live for a few hundred years. Once it reaches 40 or 50 years of age, it bears delectable nuts that are loved by bears, humans and white-breasted nuthatches. Fortunately, there are no bears at Purple Woods — at least not from what I could see — but there are a number of nuthatches. You'll recognize this endearing little bird by its distinctive *yank, yank, yank* call and its odd but effective head-first method of travelling down the tree's trunk.

Purple Woods actually takes its name from these incredible beech trees. Morning sunrises over Lake Ontario are particularly beautiful here, but the true beauty can be seen when you turn around. The warm light of morning brings the bluey-grey bark of the trees to life, and the result is a fleeting purple glow.

The sweet taste of spring.

Purple Woods is famous locally for its sugar bush. The sticky sweet tradition of maple syrup is as Canadian as plaid shirts, hockey and the great outdoors. I think maple syrup time evokes a lot of happy child-hood memories — I know it does for me. My brother and I used to wait impatiently by the wood stove for the sweet clear nectar to turn into thick, liquid gold. Even though I don't like pancakes, every spring, I seem to forget that and chow down anyway. You only live once.

Purple Woods is a great place to stop the world for a while. It sits right on the crest of the Oak Ridges Moraine and from my vantage point, I even caught a glimpse of the CN Tower. As I sat leaning against one of the elephant legs, I thought about my dad, our family signpost and the three generations of J. Eaglesons whose initials are carved into that tree. Isn't the power and beauty of a place tied to the emotions it evokes?

Why do birds sing?

Would you be surprised to know that some birds sing for the joy of it? Song is a critical form of communication for birds, and they use it for many things — to stake a territory, attract a mate, request relief from the nest, maintain the bond with their mate, call a flock together — and yes, some sing just because they like to. Listen for these songs as you hike.

red-breasted nuthatch = high nasal *ank, ank, ank or kng, kng, kng*
black-capped chickadee = *chick-a-dee-dee-dee* or *fee-bee*
red-winged blackbird = *konk-la-ree or o-ka-lay*
downy woodpecker = a flat *pick*
hairy woodpecker = a sharp *peek!*
northern cardinal = *what cheer! what cheer!*
eastern towhee = *drink your tea, drink tea*
red-shouldered hawk = high, even *kee-ah*
red-tailed hawk = harsh, descending *keeeeeer*
ovenbird = rising *teach'er, TEACHER, TEACH'ER*
black-and-white warbler = thin *weesee, weesee, weesee*

Quiet, the rock spirits are whispering.

Long Sault Conservation Area

Cycling

Birdwatching

Wildlife Viewing

Dog Sledding

Snowshoeing

Cross-country Skiing

Dogs on Leash Allowed

HIGHLIGHTS   Awesome views from high on top of the Oak Ridges Moraine. Excellent mountain biking, snowshoeing and cross-country skiing.

DIFFICULTY   Multiple Levels

TRAILS   Length: 20 km in total (Wild Bunny Run, 3 km; Norway Spruce Trail, 4.3 km; Blue Bird Trail, 3.5 km; Wild Turkey Run, 5 km; Meadowview Trail, 4.2 km)

WINTER RESTRICTIONS   The Meadowview Trail is designated for cycling, dog sledding, snowshoeing and hiking only. All other trails are open to cross-country skiing only.

SUMMER RESTRICTIONS   No bicycles are allowed on the environmentally sensitive Blue Bird Trail.

MARKERS   Cross-country ski trails are colour-coded by difficulty. Trail direction for mountain bikes are also marked. Check signs in parking lot for more details.

SURFACE   Forest paths

TYPE   Looped

FACILITIES   Parking, washrooms

OPEN   Year-round access, dawn to dusk

OWNED AND OPERATED BY
Central Lake Ontario Conservation Authority

DIRECTIONS   Exit Highway 401 at Waverly Road in Bowmanville and travel north on Regional Road 57 (Waverly) to Regional Road 20 (Concession 9). Turn right and travel east to Woodley Road. Turn left onto Woodley Road and travel north to the park entrance. To access Meadowview Trail, continue along Regional Road 20 to the East Entrance of the park.

I've always had a passion for photography. I can still remember my first camera. I think I was about ten when one of my favourite aunts gave me a black and brown 126 for Christmas. I had to stick those little square flash bulbs on the top of it and when I took a

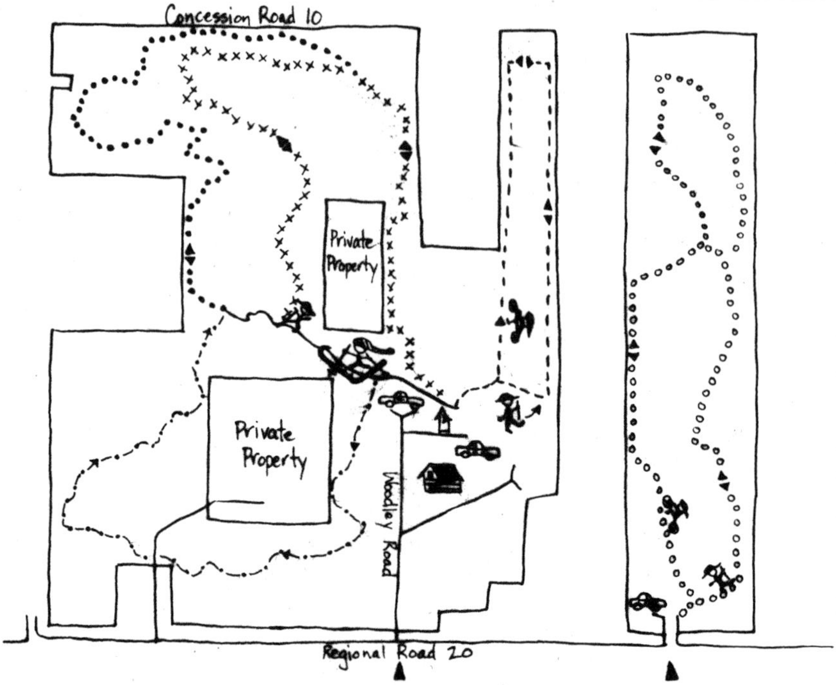

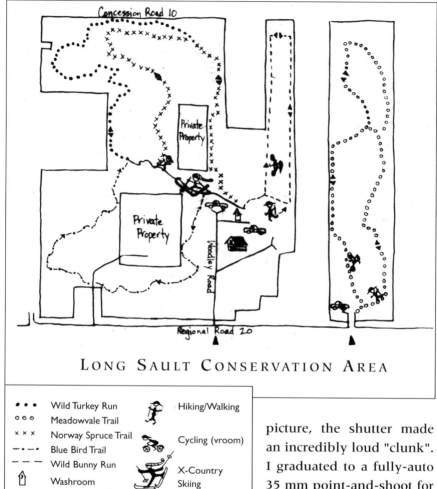

LONG SAULT CONSERVATION AREA

• • •	Wild Turkey Run	🚶	Hiking/Walking
∘ ∘ ∘	Meadowvale Trail		
× × ×	Norway Spruce Trail	🚴	Cycling (vroom)
—•—•	Blue Bird Trail		
— — —	Wild Bunny Run	⛷	X-Country Skiing
🚻	Washroom		
🏠	Chalet	🚗	Parking

picture, the shutter made an incredibly loud "clunk". I graduated to a fully-auto 35 mm point-and-shoot for my public school yearbook photos and I'm now the proud owner of a more than 20-year-old manual 35 mm camera that takes great pictures when the operator gets her act right.

Well, I have never been as inspired to take landscape photos as I was the day Rose showed me her pictures of Long Sault. The photos, which she simply called "Rock Spirit," absolutely took my breath away. The images haunted me and when I close my eyes today, I can still see them as clearly as that first day. It's almost as if she captured some kind of spirit on film, one that defies written description. The golden tones transported me to a very emotional place that I just had to discover for myself.

Long Sault is located high on the Oak Ridges Moraine, one of the most prominent and important physical features in southern Ontario. The 160-km Moraine was formed about 10,000 years ago at the end of the last ice age when retreating glaciers washed till — dirt, not a cash register — and debris into the gaps between the remaining two major ice lobes. It stretches from the Niagara Escarpment in Caledon to the Trent River east of Peterborough and is an important source of ground water for more than 30 major waterways in the region.

Standing on the crest of the Moraine just a few steps off of Long Sault's old Black Trail (now the Norway Spruce Trail), I felt the spirit that Rose had captured in her "Rock Spirit" photos. The trail wandered off past rocks that had surely been left there by the glaciers, and I shivered as I thought about the violent era that gave us these remarkably beautiful hillsides and forests. I guess it's true that something good always rises from something bad.

The beauty of the Oak Ridges Moraine.

Contrasting colours make great fall photos.

I took a few photographs from my vantage point, consciously working to avoid taking the same kind of shots Rose had shown me. I may be an amateur but I know enough about photo etiquette not to steal someone else's shot. Besides, Rose has always told me that everyone sees things a little bit differently so that's what I was aiming for.

The Norway Spruce Trail is considered Long Sault's most difficult trail and, at 4.5 km, it's a decent workout. As I hiked back to my car, a charm — neat name for a flock, isn't it? — of goldfinches flew by. They always make me smile. These beautiful yellow birds dip and sputter through the air like a plane losing power, but they always manage to get where they're going. And their favourite feast is the prickly thistle, a plant we call a weed. Beauty really is in the eye (or the beak) of the beholder.

I think I'll return to Long Sault in winter. The Meadowview Trail will be great for snowshoeing and I might even try cross-country skiing again. At the very least, I'll bring my camera. Where better to try to capture the spirit of winter than at a place created by one of the greatest winters of all?

Tips for Sharper Photos

Choose a sturdy tripod. Tripods may seem awkward out in the field but they can make the difference between crystal-clear images and fuzzy ones. Select one that extends to eye height and has thick leg sections. Ball heads are the quickest and easiest platforms for your camera.

Squeeze, don't push. Gently squeeze the shutter instead of pushing it down forcefully. Try holding your breath for sharper, hand-held photos. And if you've forgotten your cable release, try using the camera's self-timer to eliminate vibrations.

Become a human tripod. Gently cradle your lens in one hand and rest your elbows against your body. Or, sit down and rest your elbows on your knees. Don't forget about your forehead — it can make a great stabilizer.

Use a tripod for slow shutter speeds. The formula is easy. When hand-holding your lens, the slowest shutter speed you can confidently use is one divided by the length of your lens (for example, if you have a 200 mm lens, the slowest shutter speed you should use is 1/200, or 1/250 if that's the closest your camera will allow).

Frank Lloyd Wright would have been proud.

Enniskillen Conservation Area

Wildlife Viewing

Birdwatching

Fishing

Cross-country Skiing

Dogs on Leash Allowed

HIGHLIGHTS	Wonderfully quiet and free of people. Trout angler's paradise.
DIFFICULTY	Novice
TRAILS	Length: 3 km
MARKERS	Well marked
SURFACE	Footpaths with some boardwalks.
TYPE	Looped
FACILITIES	Parking, washrooms, picnic tables, recycling centres.
OPEN	Year-round access, dawn to dusk

(maintained from May through Thanksgiving).

OWNED AND OPERATED BY
Central Lake Ontario Conservation Authority

DIRECTIONS   Exit Highway 401 at Waverly Road in Bowmanville and travel north on Regional Road 57 (Waverly) to Concession 7. Turn left and travel to Holt Road. Turn right onto Holt Road, and the park entrance will be on the left.

Enniskillen is one of those parks that people seem to overlook. It doesn't have spectacular cliffs or a big lake to swim in so it often doesn't get a second glance. I know because I almost brushed it off myself. I'm glad I didn't. My favourite hiking spots are trails without a lot of people. It's not that I dislike my fellow two-legged mammals — I just like a little peace and quiet when I'm out in nature. Enniskillen is a great place for a little solitude.

Quiet places give me a chance to think. My days are a whirlwind of people, and in the frenzy of urban life, I often lose sight of myself. I struck off to Enniskillen out of obligation to complete my research for this book; I left the park with a sense of calm and a better idea about what my priorities really should be. Enniskillen was just what I needed.

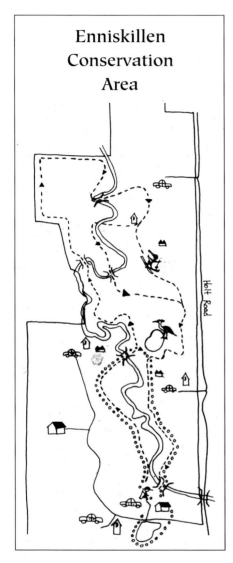

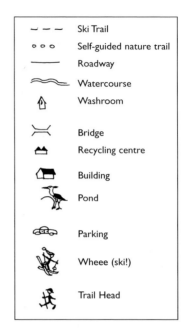

Enniskillen is filled with the simplest wonders of nature. Take, for example, the abandoned beaver dam I found spanning Bowmanville Creek, the gentle waterway that runs through the park. I'd never given dams a second thought until I looked carefully at this one. It was one of the most beautiful pieces of architecture — and art — that I'd ever seen. Beavers place gnawed trees and branches diagonally into the mud so that the wall of the dam faces downstream, and then they use their tiny paws to pack mud into their masterpiece. This ingenious construction technique braces the force of the oncoming water, creating a large reservoir of water upstream. So simple and so technically perfect.

Try as I might, however, I found no evidence of recent beaver activity. The family had probably exhausted the local food supply and moved on to greener pastures. I was saddened to think that without the loving care of its builder, this beautiful piece of art would likely break apart in the spring thaw. A word of warning when it comes to beaver dams — abandoned or not, admire them from afar. The flooded areas around them can be very dangerous, as Rose, this book's talented photographer, found out. In her attempts to get a perfect photo, she slipped thigh deep into the mud in the area. Every move she made slipped her further into the muck until she eventually  (and luckily) pulled herself free. I took her advice and stayed clear.

I chose instead to spend some time sitting in the middle of a big patch of goldenrod. I can already feel the allergy sufferers out there cringing. But no, I wasn't crazy. The tall, yellow-flowered beauty is often blamed (wrongly I might add) for much of the sneezing and sniffling during hay fever season. The real culprit is ragweed, whose pollen is swept into the skies with even the slightest breeze. Goldenrod pollen is actually sticky and is carried by the multitude of insects that are attracted to its flowers.

Abbott's sphinx caterpillar.

Life is filled with Mother Nature's generous gifts.

As I sat among the goldenrod, I noticed that the plants were scarred with tiny ball-like wounds. These tiny bulges are called galls and are one of the most remarkable examples of self-healing — and cooperation — I have ever seen. Small flies puncture goldenrod stems and lay eggs inside the plant. When the maggot-like larvae hatch, the plant immediately begins construction of new tissue around the invader, healing itself and creating a wonderful little protective hideaway for the maturing bug. The invasion of larvae clearly doesn't harm the goldenrod — some colonies of this sturdy plant have been alive for more than 100 years!

I shared my wonder at the simplicity of this process with an outdoor educator, who in turn shared a tidbit of gall information that I really didn't need to know. Apparently, those little maggot-like larvae are quite tasty and are considered a sweet treat for those who enjoy the edible wild. She denied actually eating them herself but said she had taught many a school child who had claimed the critters tasted just like brown sugar and honey. My stomach turned the same way it

Saving Green Places

Our green places are under serious threat. We are clearing away our trees, filling our swamps and wetlands, and destroying our environmentally sensitive lands — all in the name of progress and growth. These beautiful green places are critical to the survival of all of the strands of our web of life — and that means human life, too.

The Conservation Foundation and your local Conservation Authority work to stem the loss of green in Central Ontario. With the help of their many supporters, the Conservation Foundation and Conservation Authorities across the province purchase ecologically important land and make these places accessible for everyone to enjoy.

had when I watched the worm-eating scene from Star Trek, The Next Generation. Yuck. You couldn't pay me to eat one of those grubs.

On my way out of the park, I stopped to admire the life along the creek. Bowmanville Creek is one of those precious cold water streams that trout anglers salivate over. Brook and brown trout regularly make their way into Enniskillen and with a little bit of patience, you just might catch yourself a prize fish (or at least a pretty good story).

The acrobatic feeding ritual of these extraordinary fish made me stop in wonder. There were brookies everywhere I looked and to my amazement many of them were leaping completely out of the water after flying insects. I've never really considered any fish to be beautiful, but brook trout really are. The evening sunshine reflected off their athletic green bodies and their reddish fins seemed to glow in the golden light. No, it still didn't make me want to grab a rod, but the sight was remarkable. The powerful leaps and dramatic splashes are stirring to even the most ardent non-angler.

A wise friend once told me that it's the simplest things in life that mean the most, and my trek through Enniskillen reinforced that for me. Life doesn't have to be rushed — you'll enjoy it a whole lot more if you just stop from time to time and let it unfold around you.

Eastern Canada's version of a rainforest.

Heber Down Conservation Area

HIGHLIGHTS   Home to Devil's Den and the Iroquois Shoreline. Great cross-country skiing.
Wheelchair-accessible trail and fishing platform.
Wildlife viewing in the hydro corridor.

DIFFICULTY   Multiple levels

TRAILS   Length: 18 km in total (Springbanks Trail, 1 km; Iroquois Shoreline Trail, 6 km; Devil's Den, 2 km; Green Trail, 2 km; Blue Trail, 3 km; Black Trail, 4.5 km)

MARKERS   Unknown at time of printing.

SURFACE   Combination of paved surface, gravel road and footpath.

TYPE   Looped

FACILITIES   Parking, wheelchair-accessible washrooms, picnic areas.

OPEN   Year-round access, dawn to dusk (maintained from May through Thanksgiving).

OWNED AND OPERATED BY
Central Lake Ontario Conservation Authority

DIRECTIONS   Exit Highway 401 at Brock Street in Whitby and travel north on Brock to Taunton Road. Turn left onto Taunton Road and drive west to Country Lane Road. Turn right and travel to the park entrance at the end of the road.

Wheelchair and Stroller Accessible

Wildlife Viewing

Fishing

Cross-country Skiing

Photography

Dogs Allowed

Over the years, folklore has produced some truly extraordinary tales: the headless horseman, the Loch Ness monster, Bigfoot and recently, the Blair Witch Story. Not to be outdone, this book has its own little legend and you'll find it in Devil's Den at Heber Down.

Apparently, Devil's Den Lookout was a popular gathering place for pre-Confederation — that's before 1867 for the non-history buffs out there — youth to gather to swap ghost stories. Story has it that two

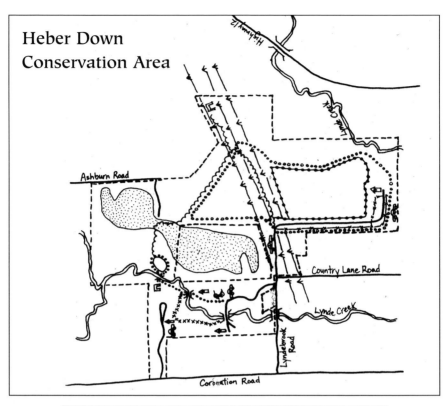

Heber Down Conservation Area

x–x–x	Green Trail	冖	Lookout
——	Roadways	～—	Watercourse
x x x	Springbanks Trail		
o o o	Black (Advanced Trail)	⚑	Washroom
●–●–●	Blue Trail	🚗	Parking
– – –	Park Boundary		
↑—↑	Hydro Line	⏝	Bridge
● ● ●	Devil's Glen Trail	♿	Wheelchair Access
∿∿	Iroquois Shoreline	▨	Sand Pits

young Victorian comedians decided to spook their buddies one day by creating their own local monster. The boys carved wildcat tracks into potatoes and proceeded to stamp a big cat trail through the valley. When their friends arrived, the boys broke into cat howls, and the group ran screaming into town.

Well, you can imagine the fright. Wildcats were not indigenous to the area so the story created quite a stir. Townsfolk even called in two expert trackers to find the big beast but they had no luck. One would think that once the cat was out of the bag (I know, that was a bad one!), the mystery would be solved. It wasn't. Locals who ventured near the valley at night would often hear the mumblings and mutterings of what sounded like human voices. These sounds, coupled with the wildcat prank, convinced everyone that the little valley was indeed possessed by the devil.

There's no need for you to worry about the horned one when you hike into Devil's Den. The voices came from local horse thieves who knew the legend would keep people out of the valley at night. Today, the trail is paved to provide access to strollers and wheelchairs, and there is nary a sound of any kind of cat — big or small.

I had to travel much further back in time — 10,000 years to be exact — to unearth the details of the Iroquois Shoreline Trail. I used to love history in elementary school, but a bad experience with a dictatorial grade nine teacher who pitched chalk at his students

A Polyphemus moth makes a rare daytime appearance.

Don't let it get away!

forever changed my perspective on the subject. Small town schools have only one history teacher, so I never took the subject again. Today, I wish I had endured.

Way back in the Pleistocene Epoch (I bet you can't say that fast three times), Ontario and the northeastern United States were covered by ice sheets. The sheets were 2-3 km thick and their carving effect forever marked our landscape. The last big glaciers retreated about 10,000 years ago, leaving behind huge meltwater lakes. Lake Iroquois covered the southern part of Ontario, upper New York State, and parts of Ohio and lower Michigan. The shoreline of this magnificent lake extended north to Heber Down, and the Iroquois Shoreline Trail follows the edge of this historic inland sea.

Eventually the water receded into the Great Lakes that we know today, but when I stood on the Lake Iroquois Shoreline Lookout at the far east end of the park, I could almost picture the woolly mammoths, grizzly bears and musk-ox that once roamed this area. It's strange to imagine that these legendary creatures actually inhabited an area now dominated by pavement and single detached homes.

As I hiked back through the hydro corridor to where my car was parked, I silently said thank you to the local Conservation Authority that had the foresight to save this unique geologic and historic gem. Until I visited this beautiful park, I hadn't even paid much attention to our powerful past. Believe me — this one is more than just a legend. It's for real.

The Art of Reading Clouds

Don't plan your weekend hike without looking up into the sky. Clouds can tell you exactly what kind of weather to expect and when. Here are a few examples:

Cirrus clouds look like feathery white brushstrokes against a beautiful blue sky. They indicate fair weather that will last for several days.

Cirrocumulus clouds look like ripples on a lake, or fish scales. These mirage-like clouds have a wet lining so plan for a day hike only.

Altostratus clouds blanket the sky, giving it a peculiar glow, and cover the sun so that it casts no shadows at all. Wet weather will arrive in 12 to 24 hours, but before it hits, take some time to enjoy the intense red, yellow or bright white sunset!

Stratus clouds look just like fog across the sky and give you a great reason to stay inside with a good book. Drizzle or snow will last for days!

Cumulonimbus clouds are dark, towering monster clouds that mean only one thing — head inside, NOW! Strong winds and heavy rains are on their way and they might just last for days.

The park comes to life after a rain.

*The equally skittish green heron and painted turtle
share a moment in the marsh.*

Lynde Shores Conservation Area / Cranberry Marsh

Birdwatching

Canoeing

Fishing

No Bicycles

No Dogs Allowed

HIGHLIGHTS   Excellent place to see migratory birds in spring and fall. Located on fall hawk migration route. Songbirds will eat out of your hands.

DIFFICULTY   Novice

TRAILS   Length: 2.25 km in total (Boardwalk, 0.25 km; Bird Feeder Trail, 0.5 km; LeVay Lane, 1.5 km). LeVay Lane is relatively new and follows the gravel road allowance to Cranberry Marsh. Please stay on the trail rather than walking on the roadway as local residents use motorized vehicles on this private road.

RESTRICTIONS: Canoeing, paddling and fishing are permitted in Lynde Marsh only. This is the marsh closest to the main park entrance.

MARKERS   None
SURFACE   Foot paths, mowed meadow and boardwalk.
TYPE   Primarily linear, Bird Feeder Trail is looped.

SPECIAL   Lynde Shores has a pay-and-display policy. Conservation Journeys members are asked to display their membership card on the car dashboard.

FACILITIES   Parking

OPEN   Year-round access, dawn to dusk

OWNED AND OPERATED BY
Central Lake Ontario Conservation Authority

DIRECTIONS   Exit Highway 401 at Brock Street in Whitby and travel south to Victoria Street (first light). Turn right and travel east approximately 2.5 km to the Lynde Shores parking lot on the south side of the road.

S omething incredible always happens whenever I visit Lynde Shores. Okay, so I've only been there three times, but each and every visit is clearly etched in my mind as if it was yesterday. And fortunately for me, there's a photographic record of each unique

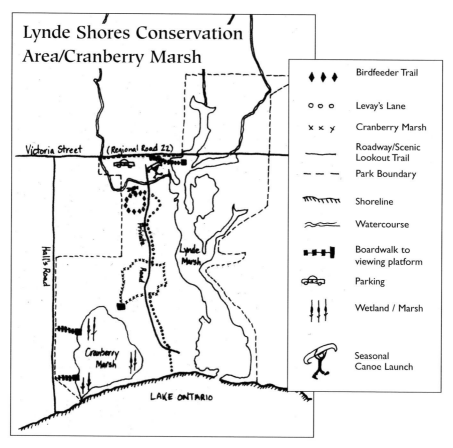

occurrence because Rose, my trusty partner in crime, was on hand to capture the moments. In fact, she's the reason why the first story even came to be.

Rose told me the only way to accurately capture the spirit of the places in this book was to experience them first-hand. With that in mind, she arranged a 5 A.M., early summer field trip to Lynde Shores. I can admit now that I wasn't all that thrilled about the sleep deprivation I was about to experience but I figured I might get some half-decent photo tips out of the excursion.

Lynde Shores is a pretty unique place. It's home to two large marshes, a woodlot, and open fields and meadows — and it extends right out to the edge of Lake Ontario. For some reason, Rose decided we should mark my first visit to the site by hiking all the way out to the lake. I think she was just trying to torture me.

The passion for fishing is sparked at a young age.

Light conversation made the 1.5 km jaunt to the lake seem much shorter than it actually was. When we reached the beach, we dropped our backpacks and paused for a light snack. We were talking about spring migration, and just as I commented that we might see some warblers, a long yodelling wail cut the air around us. Rose grabbed my arm and whispered, "Loon!"

As I rifled through my backpack for my new binoculars, Rose stood up, cupped her hands around her mouth and replicated the loon call perfectly. And the loon actually replied. If I had not been there to see it in person, I would not have believed it. A woman and a loon, in conversation, on the edge of Lake Ontario.

The common loon is probably the quintessential Canadian symbol (or at least it's right up there with the beaver, the moose and the hockey puck). This sacred bird graces our one-dollar coin and is the official bird of our beloved Ontario. For many Canadians, the haunting call of the loon brings back those wonderful childhood memories of family visits up north, of cottages and of the wilderness.

Loons have been all but driven out of southern Ontario lakes by heavy pollution, motorboat traffic, nest flooding and other key indicators of so-called human progress. But here we were, on the edge of a lake that most Ontarians view as not-so-healthy, in the company of not one but five loons. As the curious loons swam closer to investigate Rose's wails, I scanned my binoculars across the water. Yes, there were five loons — two parents and three smaller loonlings. Incredible!

Rose must have stood there talking to that loon for a good 30 minutes. The only break she took was to take a few pictures for posterity. This was my first ever experience with loons, and I was like a little kid. I pestered Rose for information on the magical birds — how deep do they dive, how long can they stay under water, how can they survive on Lake Ontario? These torpedo-like creatures can dive to depths of almost 70 metres and can stay under water for more than three minutes. And while they can out-manoeuvre most fish while they are underwater, common loons are almost helpless on land. They use their wings as crutches to help them walk the metre or so over land to their nests.

Soon, the birds determined that we were merely human and not some feathered threat to their territory. As they swam away in search of lunch, I told Rose I'd never again doubt her advice to rise early. She just laughed, and as we made our way back to the car, I asked her to teach me her amazing loon call. She laughed even harder when the only sound I could make was a weird wheezing noise. I still try to make that call, but a year and a half of practice has not made me any better. I guess it's best left to the pros.

Buoyed by our "loonie" visit to Lynde Shores, we decided to return later that summer to investigate Lynde Marsh and its wonderful boardwalk. The cattails stand taller than an adult can reach, and the walk out the boardwalk made me feel as if I was in the Deep South. Dragonflies darted around us, and a belted kingfisher screamed as he flew overhead. Up ahead, a young father patiently taught his daughter the finer points of casting.

We stood along the roadway at the creek edge and admired the birds. I caught sight of a smallish brown bird with long, yellow legs that looked a little like an old man hunched over his cane. The bird stood perfectly still on a log while a painted turtle basked in a sunbeam only a short distance away. This sighting was another first. The odd little bird with the hunch was a green heron. No, not quite as exciting as the loons but the find surely cemented my love for Lynde Shores — and for birdwatching.

I could hardly contain my enthusiasm for Lynde Shores. I told everyone I knew about the amazing things I had seen there and urged them to visit this little Eden themselves. When I shared my delight with a friend from work, she asked me if I had walked the Birdfeeder Trail, where chickadees will eat seeds right from your hand. I hadn't, and I knew I had to go back.

This time, I dragged Rose along with me at some unearthly hour. We went armed with shelled peanuts and black-oil sunflower seeds. (If you plan to try this for yourself, please take great care to bring nuts and seeds that are raw and unsalted). I wasn't even five metres onto the trail when I was buzzed by a hungry chickadee. I quickly grabbed some seeds and held my hand out. Within seconds, black-capped chickadees were dropping like paratroopers onto my hand to retrieve their tasty treats. Then, a downy woodpecker flew in for a snack. A chipmunk virtually tugged at my pant leg to ask for a peanut.

We fed our little friends for over an hour. Rose even put a peanut between her lips and the bravest chipmunk marched up and removed the morsel with his teeth. I even managed to snap a picture of that moment (it's not good enough for a book but it is good enough for a professional photographer to put on her desk at work). Lynde Shores is a great place for kids of all ages — I know because I'm one of them.

What Bird Was That?

Birdwatching is one of North America's most popular pastimes, and some birders are so skilled they can identify species in mere seconds. How do they do it? They pay close attention to these six key characteristics:

1. Size — compare the bird to ones you know well.
2. Physique — is it slender or plump, hunched or erect?
3. Bill — is the beak shaped like a needle? chisel? hook? spoon? rounded triangle? scoop? upside-down scoop?
4. Tail — is it long or short? forked or notched? rounded, square or wedge-shaped?
5. Wings — are they rounded or sharply pointed?
6. Special features — can you pick out eye rings, wing bars, tail patterns, crests, distinct colour patches?

Make a mental note of as many of these features as possible and look up your find in your favourite field guide. You could soon be an avian expert!

Petticoat's pool is larger than a football field.

Petticoat Creek Conservation Area

Swimming

Birdwatching

Photography

Snack Bar

Dogs on Leash Allowed

HIGHLIGHTS Football-field-sized swimming pool. Excellent place to spot great horned and great grey owls Bluffs along Lake Ontario.

DIFFICULTY Novice

TRAILS Waterfront Trail
LENGTH Unknown
MARKERS White with blue and green Waterfront. Trail logos.

SURFACE Paved

TYPE Linear

FACILITIES Children's playground, snack bar, change rooms, washrooms.

OPEN 9 A.M. to dusk, Victoria Day weekend to Labour Day. Pedestrian traffic only, during off-season.

OWNED AND OPERATED BY
The Toronto and Region Conservation Authority

DIRECTIONS Exit Highway 401 east at White's Road in Pickering. Travel south 1 km to the park entrance.

I decided to call her "Harriet." A rather fitting name for an owl, I thought, particularly a great horned owl. I know it may seem silly to give a human name to a wild creature, but I couldn't just call her "owl" whenever I saw her. It didn't feel right. It's hard to believe that such a rarely seen creature could live so close to humans, but there she was, just visible above the edge of her nest, in the forested corner of Petticoat Creek's property.

This urban park is best known for its enormous swimming pool (it's actually larger than a football field). I have to admit that the pool is impressive even for a non-swimmer like me. It's shallow at the edges so that toddlers — and embarrassed landlubbers — can splash to their heart's content. It deepens to just under 2 metres in the centre, providing the aquatically unchallenged an opportunity to demonstrate their talents. Best of all, the pool is staffed by certified lifeguards whose eagle eyes keep everyone safe.

Petticoat is also known for its location on top of the bluffs that line the Lake Ontario shore. The bluffs are, in a word, awesome. (Just don't get too close to the edge.) Lake Ontario's powerful waves crash against the rocky beach below, and when you look out on a clear day, you may even see the shadowy outline of buildings across the lake. Petticoat is a summer hot spot, and a number of well-manicured picnic areas can be found just north of the lake's edge.

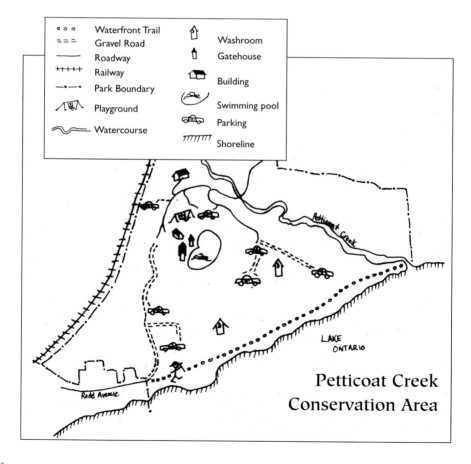

A great horned owlet ventures out to bask in the warmth of the sun.

Like those of most of the parks in this book, Petticoat's gates are closed during the winter months. But you can still walk in, and that's how I found Harriet. It's actually a lot easier to find owls by looking on the ground than by staring up into the treetops (and a lot safer for those of us who can barely walk and talk at the same time). Favourite roosts are marked by the cake-like whitewash (a really family-friendly way to say excrement) and telltale pellets (they're the regurgitated, indigestible parts of the bird's daily meals — yuck!) that accumulate under an owl's favourite roost.

Owling is really a learned activity; it is rare to find a bird without considerable patience, a handful of experience and a whole lot of luck. I've been owling for about two years now and Harriet was the first owl I'd ever actually found (until then, I'd only been lucky enough to find whitewash and empty nests).

I had some assistance the day I found Harriet. A number of trees were lined with whitewash but it was the antics of a half dozen crows in the forest ahead of me that gave Harriet's location away. It was quite a sight. There was Harriet, tightly tucked in her gnarled stick nest,

Canada geese parade along the lakefront.

with the crows taking turns dive-bombing her. Crows are aggressive attackers, and often exhaust themselves by harassing otherwise innocent owls and hawks. This was one of those moments.

I quickly knelt down a good distance away from the tree so that I wouldn't alarm the large bird (an important part of owl etiquette). I watched through my binoculars as the crows swooped in, each time getting closer and closer to Harriet's tall, feathered tufts. She didn't seem overly concerned and was clearly unwilling to budge (she was probably roosting on a clutch of eggs). I couldn't figure out the behaviour of the crows. Great horned owls are vicious predators who are known to snatch up birds, rabbits and even skunks, rip their heads from their bodies and feast on their brains. Didn't the crows know this?

Suddenly, from out of nowhere, another owl dramatically swept through the sea of crows. I could only surmise it was Harriet's mate coming to her defence. He scattered the black birds, but for only a moment; then the tables turned and the chase was on. All six crows took off after the male owl, attacking it on every perch and even during flight. I looked back at Harriet, who had bunkered even further down in her nest, and I could've sworn that she grinned as she closed her eyes. I stayed frozen in my crouch watching the circus-like proceedings for a good half an hour before the cold overwhelmed me. I vowed to return again in another month to check the nest for owlets. Now that would be a sight.

Note from the author: Take great care not to disturb an owl on her nest. Stay a good distance away and view only with binoculars or a spotting scope. Do not climb the tree or disturb the nest. Not only would you risk injury from the bird's powerful talons but you might do considerable harm to the young owlets.

Protecting the Web of Life

Protection of the delicate web of life that both surrounds us and includes us — our biodiversity — has never been more critical. Species and habitats are becoming extinct today 1000 to 10,000 times faster than the natural rate. (To put it in perspective, we haven't faced a rate of extinction like this since the time of the dinosaur.) We depend on thousands and thousands of plants, animals and microorganisms in medicine, industry, the environment and agriculture. We need to act.

The Conservation Foundation and your local Conservation Authority help provide practical solutions to protect the biodiversity of our local environment. Together, they have identified three critical areas of action to strengthen our local web of life: wildlife habitat, forests and wetlands.

They protect habitat by acquiring land, regenerating damaged habitat and monitoring key species. And they help heal the local environment by planting trees to re-establish forest canopy cover, and by regenerating wetlands.

The famous black water.

Great blue herons are patient and skilful hunters.

Beaver River Trails

		Cycling
		Birdwatching
		Photography
		Cross-country Skiing
		Snowshoeing
		Snowmobiling
		Dogs on Leash Allowed

HIGHLIGHTS   Smooth cycling for the whole family.
Awesome black water.
Lots of birdlife in the nearby wetland.

DIFFICULTY   Novice

TRAILS   Length: 17 km from Blackwater to Cannington.

MARKERS   Old rail bed is obvious.

SURFACE   Compacted, screened gravel

TYPE   Linear

OPEN   Year-round access

OPERATED BY Lake Simcoe Region Conservation Authority

DIRECTIONS   Drive north on Highway 7/12 north of Brooklin until you reach Blackwater, a concession crossing just south of the small village of Sunderland. No formal parking area is designated, but it is legal to park just off the road. There are as yet no signs indicating that it is Conservation Authority land, but the trail is easy to recognize.

I've always been a law-abiding citizen (with the exception of occasionally driving a bit too fast) so when I saw the No Trespassing sign at the Blackwater end of the Beaver River Trails, I almost stayed in my car. After a few minutes, I came to my senses. The sign had probably been put there by an overzealous snowmobiler. My brother, who is an avid sledder, once told me that some snowmobile clubs aren't as generous with their trails as his club was with theirs. A quick cell phone call to the local Conservation Authority confirmed that the trail was indeed open to the public. I went for it, and I'm glad I did.

Beaver River Trails is a multi-use trail that travels along an old rail bed between Blackwater and Cannington. It's arrow-straight and perfect for cycling. Sadly, my bike sat silent at home. It had a flat tire and I had been too lazy to patch it the weekend before. It's a good thing I had solid hiking boots because it looked like I was in for a long walk.

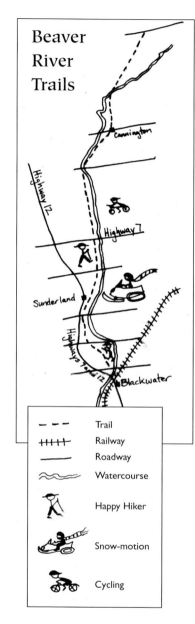

Beaver River Trails

Cannington

Highway 12

Highway 7

Sunderland

Highway 7/12

Blackwater

- - -	Trail
++++	Railway
——	Roadway
~~	Watercourse
🚶	Happy Hiker
🛷	Snow-motion
🚴	Cycling

As I crossed the rail bridge, I noticed the water. It was black — jet black — but it looked healthy enough. There were water lilies and cattails growing right in the water, and marsh marigolds were blooming along the edge of the wetland. I stood there for a while, pondering the water, until the 60-watter inside my head finally lit up — this little farming community at the end of the trail was called Blackwater. Black water. I had been a little slow that day but I'd finally gotten it. The water was black because of the type of soil that surrounded it and not because it was polluted.

I sat down on the edge of the rail bridge to contemplate the water (and my navel). I'm usually so full of nervous energy that I can't sit still for long but I still couldn't get over the colour of the water, so I parked myself there for a while. I'd managed to sit there for about 10 or 15 minutes when I realized there was a great blue heron standing as still as a statue about 50 metres away.

Great blue herons remind me of pterodactyls, those big, ugly Jurassic-like flying dinosaurs that must have terrified everything they encountered. While birds did indeed evolve from dinosaurs, great blue herons have turned out to be a whole lot prettier than their extinct ancestors. (By the way, did you know the pterodactyl wasn't even a dinosaur? Me neither until I researched this book!) Like dinosaurs, great blue herons have voracious appetites and will stop at almost nothing to satisfy their hunger pangs.

So there I was, innocently minding my own business on the edge of the bridge, when I witnessed a well-planned and bloody murder. Yes, a murder. That heron's head shot into the water at lightning speed and it emerged with a plump and juicy frog speared on its razor sharp beak. The light caught the great bird's eye, and I could've sworn that it grinned as it flipped the frog up into the air and then swallowed it whole.

That was enough for me. If the signs weren't enough, the heron's vicious ways were. I was pretty lucky though. I found out later that if a heron kills something too large for its mouth, it will simply sit with the victim hanging halfway out of its beak until it digests enough of it to fit the rest in. That's something I hope I never see.

By the way, don't be intimidated by the No Trespassing signs. The trail is beautiful and if you're on your bike, no one can catch you anyway. (Just kidding!) I think I'll head back to the trail in winter. The herons will be long gone and I know for a fact that under all of that cold weather gear, snowmobilers are just big old pussycats.

Snacking on the Trail

A well-prepared hiker always brings some munchies along for the ride, and number one on the list of snacks is often trail mix, or gorp (Good Old Raisins and Peanuts).

Commercially prepared trail mix that's readily available in the bulk aisles of most grocery stores is incredibly high in fat — a single serving provides close to 75 percent of the daily recommended intake. Healthy — and easy — high energy snacks for the trail include:

- ❁ pretzels
- ❁ reduced-fat crackers
- ❁ raisins
- ❁ bagels
- ❁ ginger snap cookies
- ❁ low-fat muffins
- ❁ fruits and veggies
- ❁ low-fat granola bars and fruit-filled cereal bars
- ❁ low-fat yogurt or pudding
- ❁ Newtons

Bring along lots of water and enjoy your trail side snacks. And try to avoid those pre-made trail mixes — there are a lot more satisfying ways to get your daily fill of fat than with them.

WEST

Wolf Lake reflects the beauty of a warm summer day.

Grandma bullfrog, queen of the wetland.

Terra Cotta Conservation Area

HIGHLIGHTS So much to see and do that
a one-day visit won't be enough.
Bird, wildlife and amphibian watcher's paradise.
Home to 37 different types of orchids,
bullfrogs the size of dinner plates and a wetland
that was once a giant swimming pool.
Located on the dramatic Niagara Escarpment.

DIFFICULTY Multiple Levels

TRAILS Length: 12 km (Main Trail, 5 km; Wolf Lake
Loop, 4 km; Novice Loop, 2 km; Spring Pond Trail, 1 km), plus
Bruce Trail winds through the park.

MARKERS Colour-coded (Main, red markers; Wolf Lake,
blue; Novice, silver; Bruce Trail, white blazes).

SURFACE Footpaths

TYPE Looped

LINKS TO Bruce Trail
Caledon Trailway

OPEN Year-round access

OWNED AND OPERATED BY
Credit Valley Conservation Authority

DIRECTIONS Travel north on Highway 10 from Brampton to Victoria. Turn
left on King Street and travel 8 km west to the village of Terra Cotta. Turn right
on Winston Churchill Boulevard and travel 2 km north to the park entrance.

Wheelchair and Stroller Accessible

Birdwatching

Wildlife Viewing

Fishing

Photography

Canoeing

Maple Syrup

Cross-country Skiing

Dogs on Leash Allowed

I thought I was having a bad dream. An enormous yellow frog
leapt into the wetland right where I was standing and scared the
daylights out of me. Yes, a yellow frog. Once I calmed down, I
crouched down to take a closer look at my evil predator. Okay, she
wasn't the foot-long monster that I thought she was, but she was the
biggest bullfrog I'd ever seen. Come to think of it, she was the first
bullfrog I'd ever seen.

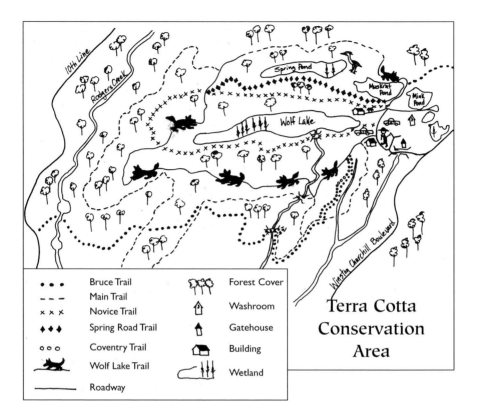

Legend:
- • • • Bruce Trail
- – – – Main Trail
- x x x Novice Trail
- ♦ ♦ ♦ Spring Road Trail
- ○ ○ ○ Coventry Trail
- Wolf Lake Trail
- Roadway
- Forest Cover
- Washroom
- Gatehouse
- Building
- Wetland

Terra Cotta
Conservation
Area

I think she must have been the grandma of Terra Cotta's Spring Pond. Her sides were bulging with eggs and she was easily the size of small dinner plate. As I got down on all fours to get a frog's eye view, she once again leapt and this time, so did I. If anyone was watching, they would have thought I was crazy. There I was, a grown woman, with my nose a half a metre from a frog.

Bullfrogs are Ontario's largest frog, growing to a maximum length of 23 cm. (That's a whopping nine inches for those of you who haven't made the conversion yet.) They are well known for their voracious appetites and will devour just about anything they can subdue, including bats and small birds that fly too close to the water's surface.

A few decades ago, every child who caught a frog proudly took it home to mom. Sadly, Ontario's bullfrog population is in decline, and unless the trend reverses most children will soon never be able to see one. Amphibians such as frogs, newts and salamanders are key indicators of a healthy environment for other plants and animals, including humans. Early death of our amphibious friends can raise serious alarms about the presence of unwanted chemicals in the water we drink, the air we breathe and the soil where we grow our food.

Enough of the serious stuff. So there I was, on my hands and knees, trying to commune with grandma bullfrog. Clearly, I just didn't have the right touch and she sploshed off again, this time further out into the pond. I think I'll consult with a frog expert before I try that again.

Terra Cotta is home to an incredible number of birds and animals, including white-tailed deer, coyote, red fox, great horned owls, rough-legged hawks, ruby-throated hummingbirds and turkey vultures. Turkey vultures are elegant flyers that are beautiful to watch — when they're in the air. Look up, and you'll recognize their unique features right away. The underside of their 2-metre wingspan has a distinctive grey-black pattern, and they seem to soar effortlessly, rarely flapping their wings.

On the ground, turkey vultures are not quite so attractive to look at. They have bright-red, bald heads that only a mother could love, and their favourite feast is roadkill. Unlike most other birds, they use their keen sense of smell to locate their meals and once they've locked onto a scent, they keep an eye out for it by "looking" down through their giant nostrils. Wait, it gets better. If you get too close to one of their nests, they may vomit the disgusting contents of their stomach toward you and then feign death. A naturalist friend (and I use the word friend loosely) once suggested I go out and lie motionless in a field so I could see a turkey vulture up-close and personal. Right.

Don't get me wrong — I love birdwatching, just not when there's vomit involved. I started birdwatching about four years ago and made my binocular investment two years later. Yes, it is truly an investment, but the clarity of a good pair of binoculars makes species identification so much easier. So, armed with my trusty field guide and my beloved binoculars, I struck off along Terra Cotta's Main Trail on a bird hunt.

The complete Main Trail hike is about four kilometres long, so I allowed myself about an hour and a half for all the inevitable stops and starts I knew I'd have. I was about a half an hour into my hike when I heard a crow commotion up ahead. I stopped to properly orient myself to the sound and then struck off toward the cawing.

The Bruce Trail attracts both casual and serious hikers.

You'll almost always find something interesting going on when you follow the caw of the crow. As I mentioned before, these big, fearless birds will spend hours pestering and chasing hawks and owls. In fact, it seems they won't stop until they've tired themselves out with the effort. This instance was no different. Four or five crows were frantically trying to knock what looked to be a bigger crow off a nearby tree branch. As I raised my binoculars to my eyes, I caught a glimpse of the trademark hooked beak of a bird of prey and my heart skipped a beat. This diminutive hawk (by hawk standards) had wide alternating black and white bands on its tail and a red breast. It was a broad-winged hawk.

Broad-winged hawks are extremely rare in the Toronto region and only 6 of these majestic creatures have been confirmed in that area. They are so rare that they have been listed as a species of concern by Toronto and Region Conservation. This was the first broad-wing I had ever seen and I was mesmerized. I watched in awe as the crows took turns diving and buzzing the hawk, trying to knock him off his perch. At first, he seemed unconcerned — he just wanted to finish the lunch he had clutched in his talon. Before long, his patience grew thin and he flew off with the crows in hot pursuit.

The rest of my bird search was uneventful but that was perfectly fine with me. My day had already been made. As I floated my way back to the car, I was already daydreaming about the bird tales I could tell my friends. By the time I got home, the story was already more dramatic and more dangerous than in reality, with dozens of crows circling above a vicious, screaming hawk. I figure that's okay though. Everyone needs a good fish — I mean bird — story now and then.

The red eft is the immature stage of the Eastern Newt.

Beware of poison ivy!

The battle with poison ivy is one you likely won't win. The itching, burning patch of red on your skin can actually get so bad that it becomes painful. And don't be smug just because you think you're immune to it now; your tolerance to this nasty ivy changes with age. Your reaction might get better but more likely it will get worse. It seems that some can break out in little red poison ivy bumps without even being near a plant!

Poison ivy is easy to identify from these three characteristics:

1) the plant has three shiny leaflets to a leaf, with the back two joined tightly together to the stem;
2) the triangular leaflets have saw-toothed edges and pointed tips; and
3) small grey or white "berries" grow on the stem behind the leaves.

If you discover you've hiked through an area with poison ivy, take action immediately. Wash any bag, equipment or skin that has come into contact with the irritating plant. Wash your clothes thoroughly and whatever you do, don't touch your pants and then your face. Over-the-counter ointments and anti-histamines may be necessary to keep you sane if you do develop a rash.

My canoe and I are changed by water.

Heart Lake Conservation Area

Swimming

Birdwatching

Fishing

Photography

Canoeing

Cross-country Skiing

Tobogganing

Dogs on Leash Allowed

HIGHLIGHTS   Lake well stocked with rainbow trout.
Great place for swimming and family canoeing.
Dense forest shuts out the outside world.
Great place to see waterfowl in spring.

DIFFICULTY   Intermediate

TRAILS   Length: 8 km
MARKERS   Yes
SURFACE   Footpath
TYPE   Looped

FACILITIES   Canoe and pedal boat rentals, change rooms, washrooms, children's playground.

OPEN   Summer: end of April to Thanksgiving, 9 A.M. to dusk.
Pedestrian traffic only, during off-season.

OWNED AND OPERATED BY
The Toronto and Region Conservation Authority

DIRECTIONS   From Highway 401, travel north on Highway 410 to Brampton. Highway 410 turns into Heart Lake Road at Bovaird Drive. Continue north approximately 3 km from Bovaird Drive to the park entrance.

The masked marauder basked in the sun in its nap spot high over my head. I probably would never have spotted it if I hadn't stopped to tie up my boot lace and take a look around. Much to the surprise of many urban dwellers who think they have the monopoly on these night raiders, raccoons actually can live and thrive in the wild, like here at Heart Lake.

Raccoons are brazen thieves, often raiding garbage cans and campsites for fine cuisine. They may even invade your home or garage to raise their young. As I stood looking up at this innocent looking cutie, I was reminded of a dear friend's predicament with a furry bandit, her

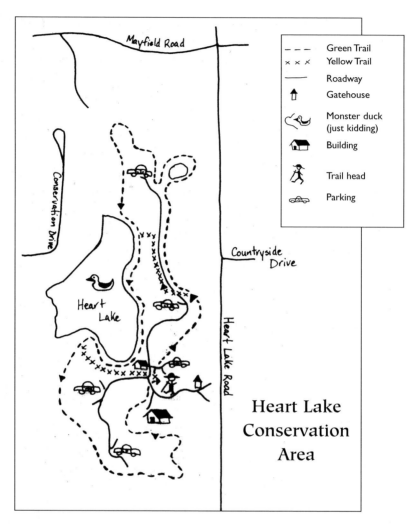

Heart Lake
Conservation
Area

cubs and the family's chimney. After weeks of an ever-increasing foul aroma, my friend humanely coaxed the critters out, using bright lights and non-stop talk radio. (Now, how humane was that?)

Raccoons are extremely intelligent and have incredibly sensitive front paws. Their front paws actually have thousands more nerve endings than our hands do. They are driven by a wild curiosity and will use their dextrous fingers to nimbly pick up everything around them. The compulsive food-washing we immediately associate with raccoons isn't actually washing. They dip just about everything in the cold stuff because water apparently heightens their sense of touch.

(No wonder they seem to be able to pluck crayfish and frogs from their underwater lairs without really paying attention.)

The Heart Lake forests are filled with tall, wide-crowned red oaks. (That's where I found my masked buddy.) These notch-leafed trees are widely known as thunder trees because their large crowns make them susceptible to lightening strikes. This predisposition has given them a significant position in ancient folklore. (Didn't Zeus live in an oak tree?)

Red oaks are actually more colourful in spring than in fall. Tannins gives the trees' waxy new leaves a distinct red colour — and a bitter-tasting defence against animal browsing. And like the peculiar goldenrod galls at Enniskillen, oak leaves and branches have their own bizarre tumours. Wasps lay their eggs on oak leaves and the hatched larvae munch their way into the leaves. Like the goldenrod, the oak fights back, immediately building dense tissue around the offender. I glanced at a leaf on a young sapling and counted seventy-nine tiny, brown galls. (No, I didn't eat any of these galls either — they're probably poisonous as well as unappetizing!) It makes you wonder how many galls you'd find on a hundred-year-old tree.

In search of an adventure.

The masked marauder.

In fall, the delectable acorns attract deer, raccoons, squirrels, chipmunks, nuthatches, blue jays and even wood ducks. Wood ducks bring true meaning to the phrase "odd duck." They have peculiar claws on their feet that allow them to perch in trees and, unlike most other ducks, they much prefer acorns and berries to crustaceans.

I've never seen a wood duck at Heart Lake, but the habitat sure seems right — thick, vegetation-lined shores with mature trees nearby. The lake itself is a staging area for waterfowl and plenty of non-resident northern beauties. Common mergansers are familiar visitors on their trip to nest in the northern lakes of the Canadian shield. I have a particular fondness for these swift-flying birds — and I don't even care that they look like lawn darts when they fly. I watch our local lakes every spring for a glimpse of them.

Heart Lake is a lot like Toronto's High Park (it's just a lot better-kept secret). The dense forests shut out the outside world and once you're inside, you feel like you're hours from the city. And while this park doesn't have a zoo, restaurant, tennis courts or outdoor theatre like its downtown cousin, Heart Lake does boast a sand beach, excellent fishing and peaceful canoeing on its large lake.

I'm embarrassed to say that I'd completely overlooked Heart Lake (and even travelled to High Park) when I lived in Brampton. That's a whole lot different now. The first day I visited Heart Lake was the last time I even thought about making the long trek to that famous Toronto park. I'm glad I came to my senses. Besides, Heart Lake is a jewel that very few people know about. I get a real sense of the wild when I'm inside its fences. Who could ask for anything more?

The Early Bird Gets the Worm

It's often difficult to drag yourself out of the comfort of a warm bed before 5 A.M. But once you're up and in the great outdoors, you'll discover that the early bird really does get the worm.

In summer, most birds and mammals are more active between 5 and 8 A.M. than at any other time of day. A great place to see wild creatures is near a source of water, particularly a river. A river deposits material on its inside bends, creating a stony bar or island. Wildlife like deer, raccoon and mink come to drink or hunt in the shallow area just downstream from the bar. Find a quiet spot downwind to sit and watch the action around the water — you never know what you might see.

Zen and the art of fly-fishing.

Belfountain Conservation Area

Birdwatching

Fishing

Photography

Swimming

Dogs On Leash Allowed

HIGHLIGHTS   Home to a mini-Niagara Falls, a Yellowstone-like artificial cave, a suspension bridge and a stone foundation. Steep, challenging trails along the Niagara Escarpment. In the heart of one of Ontario's prettiest fall colour areas. Trout fishing in the beautiful Credit River.

DIFFICULTY   Intermediate

TRAILS   Length: 1 km (Head Pond Trail, 0.4 km; River Trail, 0.6 km)

MARKERS   None

SURFACE   Very steep footpaths

TYPE   Looped

LINKS TO   Bruce Trail
Forks of the Credit Provincial Park
(via the Bruce Trail)
Elora Cataract Trailway

OPEN   Open late April to October. Pedestrian traffic is prohibited in the off-season due to unsafe conditions.

FACILITIES   Parking, picnic tables

OWNED AND OPERATED BY   Credit Valley Conservation Authority

DIRECTIONS   Travel north on Highway 10 from Brampton to the Forks of the Credit Road (Peel Road 11). Turn left and travel 7 km west to the Village of Belfountain. The park is on your left as you enter the village. The Forks of the Credit Road is narrow and winds dramatically through the Credit River valley. Please drive slowly and watch for tourists and pedestrians.

I'm convinced that great things happen in the rain. Let me rephrase that — great memories are made when it rains. Everything seems more dramatic, more energizing, when it's raining. I have kayaked alongside breeching whales during an intense evening drizzle. I have sat and watched the drama unfold as waves and storm

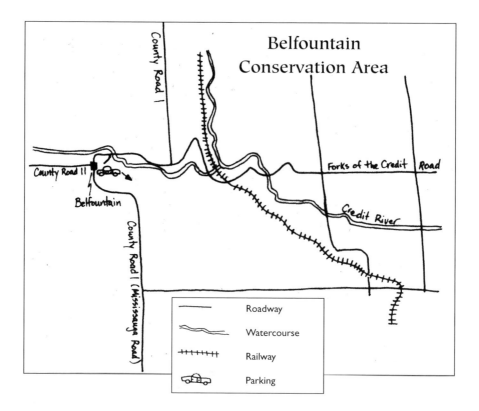

clouds crashed across the north channel of Lake Huron. I have quietly and reverently participated in the rituals of a First Nations sunrise ceremony during an early fall cloudburst. And I have stood beside a very wet dog with a stopwatch in my hand, counting out the right number of seconds to capture the perfect exposure for a fall photograph in Belfountain Conservation Area.

You might be thinking that memories of a stinking dog in a downpour wouldn't stack up against the others I mentioned, but you'd be wrong. Belfountain Conservation Area is best described as wild and weird (that's weird in a good way). Its former owner was a mite eccentric and he actually tried to re-create some of his favourite landforms — like Niagara Falls — right on his property.

Charles W. Mack, the inventor of the rubber stamp, purchased the land in 1908 and promptly hired a local stonecutter to craft the Niagara Falls-like waterfall (don't worry, it's not nearly that big), an artificial cave that's designed after those found in Yellowstone National Park, and a large stone fountain. He later added a suspension bridge beside the waterfall and a number of trails that ramble and scramble up and down the steep edge of the Niagara Escarpment.

I'm actually ashamed to admit that even though I once lived in the village of Belfountain, I never once visited this remarkable little spot when I lived there. Could this be what the old "not in my backyard" theory really means? I clearly know better now. I've now visited it many times over the past few years but no visit punctuates my memory the way my most recent one does.

I should have recognized the cloud forms before I drove to Belfountain that day, but the pull of one of Ontario's premiere fall colour destinations overcame my better judgement. The village of Belfountain is a busy little tourist spot that welcomes well over 10,000 people every weekend during the fall colour season. Despite the presence of those stratus clouds, people were flocking to town in waves. Rose gently reminded me that wet weather actually makes fall colours seem more intense. That's where the stopwatch came in.

Wet weather can damage your camera equipment.
Keep an old shower cap in your bag, cut a hole for your eyepiece and wrap
the elasticized edges around to keep the top of your lens dry.

*A quiet moment
on the swing bridge.*

The rain hadn't started when we embarked on our hike but those clouds sure weren't lifting. Stratus clouds are easy to identify when you aren't swayed by the romance of the crimsons, coppers, russets and ochres of fall. These clouds are light to dark grey and look a lot like fog across the sky. Occasionally, the sun might peek through, but stratus clouds usually carry with them a light drizzle that could last for days. Stratus clouds are a good excuse to curl up with a good book. (If only I'd paid attention to them before I left home!)

Rose's big black lab was so excited about our hike that she almost dragged me right into the river. Belfountain's trails are mighty steep and if I had it to do over again, I'd think twice about taking an excited dog along. We made our way over the bridge and struck off into the woods in search of the perfect scene.

Well, the rain hit when we reached the bottom of the trail. The colours along the river seemed to pop off the trees and the mist created a surreal scene — a scene that Rose couldn't turn her back on. As she slipped and stumbled in her search for the perfect angle, I tried my best to take refuge from the rain. It wasn't a pretty sight: my camera bag, her camera bag, my tripod and one very wet dog. It's a good thing I had my waterproof canvas hat on.

The scene called for long exposures of five, ten and even fifteen seconds and I was the only one with a watch. I stepped out into the rain, held my hand high in the air and yelled out ONE, TWO, THREE... as I raised each finger.

Yes, the pictures were worth it, as you can see. Just one word to the wise: please take extreme care on Belfountain's steep trails, particularly when they're wet. I slipped and twisted my hip in the transition between boardwalk and mud, and I limped my way out under the weight of my gear. So, no, it's not quite the same memory as the whales or the sunrise ceremony, but it's a memory nonetheless. And it's as firmly etched in my mind as the others.

Go for the Colours

Autumn is a magical time. A kaleidoscope of spectacular colours and relatively mild temperatures brings "leaf-peepers" and nature photographers out to enjoy the scenery. But how can you possibly know what colours you'll find once you arrive at a destination? Easy! This list takes some of the guesswork out of finding the colours you love most.

sugar maple = yellow, orange or scarlet
red maple = yellow, orange or scarlet
silver maple = pale yellow
American beech = yellow and brown
white oak = red or brown
red oak = scarlet
black walnut = yellow
shagbark hickory = golden brown
white elm = bright yellow
sassafras = yellow, orange or red
white birch = light yellow
white ash = purple or yellow
eastern cottonwood = yellow
trembling aspen = golden yellow
largetooth aspen = golden yellow
staghorn sumac = scarlet, orange and yellow

*A dramatic valley, complete with a waterfall and the remains
of an old grist mill, marks the east end of the trail.*

Elora Cataract Trailway

Wheelchair and Stroller Accessible

Cycling

Birdwatching

Horseback Riding

Photography

Snowmobiling

Snowshoeing

Cross-country Skiing

Wildlife Viewing

Dogs on Leash Allowed

HIGHLIGHTS   Long distance trail on former CP rail bed. Spectacular Cataract Falls at the Forks of the Credit. Provincial Park lies at the east end of the trail; awesome Elora Gorge marks the western end of the trail. Great for bicycles. Great photo spots.

DIFFICULTY   Intermediate

TRAILS   Length: 47 km
MARKERS   None (old rail bed is clearly visible)
SURFACE   Compacted screened gravel
TYPE   Linear

LINKS TO   Bruce Trail
                  Grand Valley Trail

OPEN   Year-round access

MANAGED BY Credit Valley Conservation Authority

DIRECTIONS   Travel north on Highway 10 from Brampton. Turn left and travel west on Peel County Road 24 (formerly Highway 24) to Erin. Turn left onto Ross Street and you'll find the Erin access point at the corner of Ross and Daniels Streets. You can travel either west or east from here. Parking along streets and roads closer to Cataract is closely monitored due to high volumes of tourist traffic in the area. Don't be towed! Park in Erin and make your way back east.

T ake it from me — don't attempt a 75 km bicycle trip for your second ride of the season. Yes, the path may be relatively flat, and yes, the passing countryside might be beautiful, but your body will ache afterwards and you'll be walking funny for a week. Trust me, I know.

I shared the journey — and the pain — with Rose, who hoisted her 12 kg camera bag onto her back just in case we came upon something worth shooting. Maybe I shouldn't have complained quite so much about my discomfort...

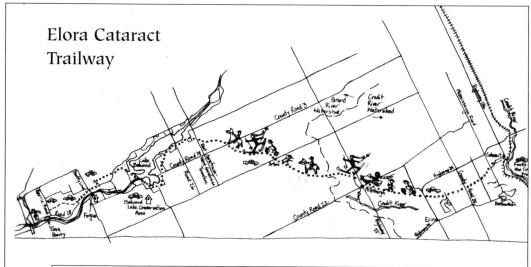

Elora Cataract Trailway

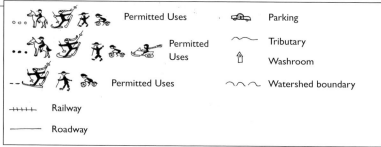

Permitted Uses	Parking	
Permitted Uses	Tributary	
Permitted Uses	Washroom	
Railway	Watershed boundary	
Roadway		

We unloaded our bikes in Erin and backtracked east to the Cataract end of the trail. What a view. Just inside the edge of Forks of the Credit Provincial Park, the Credit River cuts through the Niagara Escarpment and crashes over an incredible waterfall. This was definitely worth shooting.

I love photography, and my many adventures with Rose have given me a wealth of helpful ideas to improve my own pictures. I'll never be able to see like her or create art the way she can, but I have fun taking pictures and for me, that's really what matters. By the time we mounted our bikes to head west, the sun had already climbed high in the sky. It was time to slap on the sun screen.

The Elora Cataract Trailway is a 47-km, multi-use trail that was built on a former Canadian Pacific rail bed. The trail is pretty much arrow straight for much of its length, and its smooth surface makes for easy cycling — except on the day we rode it. The short section that connects Erin to Hillsburgh felt more like a washboard than anything else. I tried to remember all of those cycling tips that are supposed to help reduce the impact of the trail — weight forward, elbows bent, hands loose, knees bent, bum slightly off the seat — but I have to admit that I was ready to give up after the first few kilometres. I'm glad I didn't.

The trail improved dramatically once we made Hillsburgh, so we continued westward. In fact, the terrain improved so much that we lost track of time and distance. Before long, we found ourselves about 3 km outside Fergus — and over an hour away from the car. As tempted as we were to press on to the Elora Gorge, we knew we should head back. We decided to save the century (a 100-km ride) for a day when our legs and lungs were stronger.

The scenery along the trailway is really quite varied. At Belwood, you can test your speed — and your fitness — by trying to outrace the speedboats on the nearby Grand River. Between Belwood and Orton, the trail cuts through open farmland; between Orton and Hillsburgh,

Don't forget to stop to take in the view.

The author throws herself into the fireweed.

the path passes through hardwood forests that form an inviting canopy of leaves over the trail.

A patch of brilliant pink fireweed caught our eyes somewhere near the East-West Garafraxa Townline, and we stopped to take some photos. After considerable pleading and with a reward of ice cream within my grasp, I consented to pose in the midst of these tall flowers. Fireweed showcases the earth's remarkable ability to regenerate itself. As you might suspect from its name, fireweed is one of the first plants to rise from areas blackened by fire. After a few years, the flower is overtaken by fast-growing tree saplings, but by then, the wind will have carried the 45,000-plus seeds produced annually by each plant to new homes. As you can see, the photos look great and believe me, the ice cream tasted even better. I'm still not sure it was enough of a reward considering the number of thistles I had to fight through even to get to the fireweed (not to mention the sore aching muscles). Maybe next time, I'll hold out for some homemade cherry tarts from the bakeshop in Erin.

Actions Speak Louder than Words

Conservation Authorities:

* manage and protect the quality and the availability of our most vital natural resource — water

* plant trees to help remove the CO_2 in the air we breathe and protect the world from the threat of global warming

* turn ugly patches of concrete into living, breathing, community parks

* regenerate wetlands to provide vital habitat for the unique plants, birds, animals and insects that live there

* solve serious shoreline erosion problems

* rehabilitate streams so that salmon, trout and other fish can reach their spawning grounds and birds, mammals, insects and humans can enjoy healthy, clean water

* acquire and protect environmentally sensitive lands

* review development, zoning, building and land division plans with an eye to preserving biodiversity

* construct trails and provide much-needed public access to green places and green spaces

* connect wild areas to ensure that wildlife, amphibians and birds have safe corridors for travel

* educate school children, new Canadians, adults and community groups on conscientious ways to make a difference in our environment

* partner with public and private groups to effect real change on the regional environment

Mallards put on a show.

Island Lake Conservation Area/Orangeville Reservoir

Birdwatching

Fishing

Photography

Swimming

Canoeing

Windsurfing

Snowshoeing

Maple Syrup

Boat Launch

Dogs on Leash Allowed

Boat Rentals

Cross-country Skiing

Ice Fishing

Ice Skating

Wildlife Viewing

HIGHLIGHTS   Fantastic spot for summer watersports.
Provincially significant wetlands. Ice fishing mecca.

DIFFICULTY   Intermediate

TRAILS   Length: 5.5 km (Shoreline Trail, 1 km;
Sugar Bush Trail, 2 km; Plantation Trail,
1 km; Old Meadow Trail, 1.5 km).

MARKERS   Colour-coded (blue, red, green, yellow).

SURFACE   Footpaths and mowed meadow.

TYPE   Looped

FACILITIES   Parking, washrooms

OPEN   WINTER: December to mid-March
SUMMER: end of April to end of October

OWNED AND OPERATED BY
Credit Valley Conservation Authority

DIRECTIONS   Travel north on Highway 10 from Brampton
to Orangeville. Turn right at Buena Vista Drive (second set of
lights) and travel east to Hurontario Street (second street).
Turn left onto Hurontario and drive north to the park entrance.

I once made the mistake of joking with an aquatic biologist that "A
duck is a duck is a duck." (That was before I became an avid
birder, of course.) Well, twenty minutes later and with my tail
clearly tucked between my legs, I retreated to the safety of my car to
lick my wounds. My head was filled with the finer subtleties of ducks,
shorebirds, colonial waterbirds and everything in between. Not only
did I learn the ins-and-outs of waterbirds, but I also walked away
with a mental note that I should never joke with someone who takes
the avian world so seriously.

I tested my waterbird knowledge during a late spring walk-about
at Island Lake. Everyone knows the early birder gets the best sightings
so I had stumbled out of bed long before sunrise try to catch the best

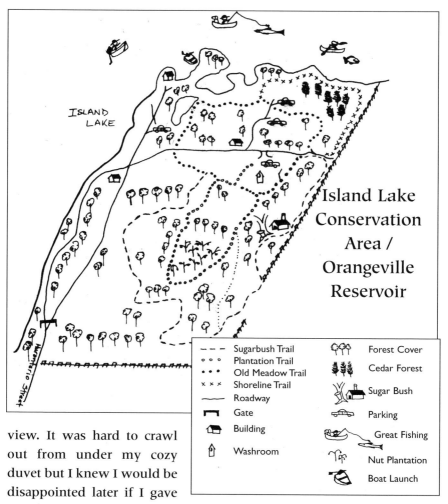

ISLAND
LAKE

Island Lake
Conservation
Area /
Orangeville
Reservoir

– – –	Sugarbush Trail	🌲🌲🌲	Forest Cover
∘ ∘ ∘	Plantation Trail	🌲🌲🌲	Cedar Forest
• • •	Old Meadow Trail		Sugar Bush
x x x	Shoreline Trail		
——	Roadway		Parking
⌐	Gate		Great Fishing
🏠	Building		
🚾	Washroom		Nut Plantation
			Boat Launch

view. It was hard to crawl out from under my cozy duvet but I knew I would be disappointed later if I gave in to the comforts of home. I even made myself a coffee (truly peculiar behaviour for a non-caffeine drinker) to stimulate my tired soul.

Island Lake is more of a reservoir than a lake. It was constructed in 1969 to store spring run-off for gradual release into the Credit River throughout the summer months. It has become a home to a variety of fish, birds and mammals and a playground for water-loving recreationists, including anglers, swimmers, windsurfers, canoeists and rowers. I left the canoe at home and came armed with my binoculars, a field guide and my trusty boots. This was to be a land-based adventure.

To my surprise, the gates were open and the parking lot was packed when I arrived at 6:30 A.M. Conservation Areas are rarely open before 8 A.M. so I was a tad confused — and I will say disappointed — by the presence of so much humanity. So much for birdwatching in silence. The enthusiastic young fellow in the gatehouse greeted me with a cheerful, "Ready to tackle a pike?" to which all I could muster was a rather dumb, "Uhhhh, no!" He quickly filled me in on the packed parking lot. I had arrived on day two of the Tackle a Pike Fishing Derby and there were already over 100 anglers on the lake vying for some top-notch prizes. My warm bed was looking pretty nice right now.

As I locked up my car and struck off toward the Shoreline Trail, I re-evaluated the situation. Serious anglers are extremely quiet people so maybe the birds I hoped to see would still be hanging around. As I approached the tiny wetland at the end of the trail, I startled a pair of ducks who beat a hasty retreat. By the time I grabbed my binoculars and focused, the birds were long gone. Were they mallards or black ducks? Mallard drakes (males) have that typical green head, and the hens are brown with a distinctive wing bar. Black drakes and hens are, just that — black or a very dark brown, with lighter heads, a blue wing patch and a white underwing that's visible only in flight. My instincts told me that I had seen a mallard drake but I thought I'd also seen some sort of white flash as they flew away.

Both breeds are almost genetically identical and it's quite common

The lake is busy from morning until night.

Thankfully, some non-native plants (like this lily-of-the-valley) are not invasive.

for the two species to interbreed — apparently the black hens seem to prefer flashier men. Unfortunately, the cross-breeding has resulted in a significant decline of black ducks, particularly in the southern half of Ontario.

I parked myself on the edge of the water and scanned the shore with my binoculars. Not many birds in sight, but there were lots of anglers. Most were patiently casting their lines out, hoping to catch the big one. As I settled in to wait for a catch, I noticed a man standing in a canoe, fly-fishing for his pike. My fascination with fly fishing started with everyone's favourite Redford flick, *A River Runs Through It*. I will admit that the back view I had wasn't nearly as romantic as the movie, but the thought of landing a feisty pike with a fly rod intrigued me.

I sat and watched the fly fisher and his buddy take turns standing up to try their luck. There's something very stirring about the elegance of a perfect cast and the silence of wide open spaces. Hey, it almost made me want to try fishing. Then I remembered those ugly hooks and the sad looks I was convinced the fish had when they were yanked from the water. I gave my head a quick shake and decided to head off toward the dam. A local naturalist had apparently spotted an osprey nest at that end of the lake and after all, I was here to see the birds.

Ospreys are phenomenal birds. These giant fish hawks have wing spans that can reach close to six feet and the sight of an osprey diving out of the sky like a bullet to catch a fish is nothing short of breath-taking. Ospreys are often mistaken for bald eagles, but the two are easily differentiated by wing structure. Bald eagles have broad, straight wings; ospreys have crooked wings that look almost like elbows.

A falconer who raised birds of prey once told me that there's something else that clearly differentiates an eagle and an osprey. Both birds can dive out of the air to catch a fish but only the osprey can release it if it's too big for the bird to land it. The falconer told of a story of a west coast angler who fought for an hour to land what he thought was an enormous salmon, only to discover a drowned eagle still attached to the fish's back. Once it wraps its powerful talons around its prey, an eagle cannot let it go until it lands and relaxes a bit. Perhaps eagles should stick to scavenging — it sure seems safer!

I wandered around Island Lake for quite some time, searching for the osprey. I found neither the bird nor its distinctive nest, and I soon left thinking that the naturalist had perhaps dreamed the entire story up. It would make quite a good fish story, wouldn't it?

Snowshoes Spell Winter Freedom

Snowshoes don't actually let you walk on top of the snow. They allow you to float on the snow and keep you from sinking very far. There are two basic types of snowshoes: the traditional, made with wood and rawhide, and the modern, made with more high-tech materials including aircraft aluminum, plastic and rubber.

Traditional wood and rawhide snowshoes evoke the romance of our country's first peoples. These snowshoes are often wide and long, providing a large base and excellent stability for parents toting a baby carrier. Traditional snowshoes are ideal for flat and even country trails that are not marked with snowmobile ruts or littered with logs and rocks.

Modern snowshoes are best suited to rough and hilly terrain. These shoes are usually narrower and shorter than traditional snowshoes, and some users feel they are easier to walk with than traditional models. They often feature crampons, or cleats, that give a good grip when you walk on a slope.

*This stone fence marks the edge of the Niagara Escarpment
and the Oak Ridges Moraine.*

Glen Haffy Conservation Area

Birdwatching

Fishing

Photography

Dogs on Leash Allowed

HIGHLIGHTS	Stocked trout ponds.
	Fantastic fall colours.
	Home to one of the world's largest corn mazes.
DIFFICULTY	Multiple Levels
TRAILS	Length: 6 km (Red Trail, 2.7 km; Green Trail, 0.9 km; Blue Trail, 2.3 km) plus Bruce Trail.
MARKERS	Colour-coded arrows
SURFACE	Footpaths with some boardwalk steps.
TYPE	Looped
LINKS	Bruce Trail
FACILITIES	Parking, picnic areas, washrooms, bait shop.
SEASONAL	Last Saturday in April to Thanksgiving, 9 A.M. to dusk.
	Pedestrian traffic only, during off-season.

OWNED AND OPERATED BY
The Toronto and Region Conservation Authority

DIRECTIONS Travel north from Brampton on Airport Road. Glen Haffy is located 10 km north of the village of Caledon East.

This time, I really knew I was crazy. For some reason, I had let Rose talk me into getting into a helicopter to get a bird's eye view of the Glen Haffy corn maze. "It'll be great," she exclaimed. "I fly like this all the time." My flight hours were limited and I wondered how similar it might be to the bumpy, forty-minute spin I took as a child in my uncle's single engine, two-seater.

To my surprise, this flight was a whole lot smoother than that last ride in a small aircraft, but I think I still prefer terra firma. Still, I must admit that seeing an aerial view of the world's largest maze gave me whole new perspective on corn fields. It was impressive. The staff at Glen Haffy spend six long months designing, planting and nurturing

Nature
HIKES

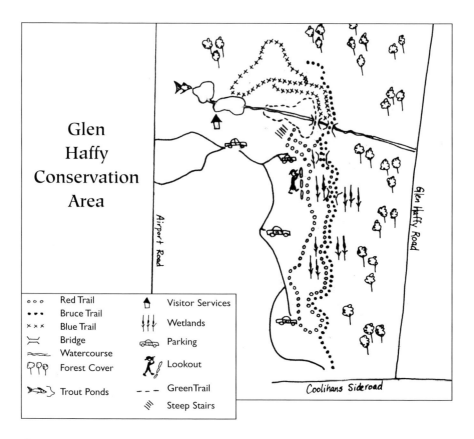

Glen Haffy Conservation Area

o o o	Red Trail	🚩	Visitor Services
• • •	Bruce Trail		
× × ×	Blue Trail		Wetlands
⋈	Bridge	🚗	Parking
∼	Watercourse		
🌳🌳🌳	Forest Cover	🧍	Lookout
🐟	Trout Ponds	- - -	Green Trail
		⫽⫽	Steep Stairs

the giant maze in preparation for their fall extravaganza. And it's definitely worth the effort.

The only way most people will get the view I had is through Rose's photos. But there are plenty of other ways to explore these enormous mazes. The view from the ground is no less impressive, as I soon found out. I received my instructions before I entered the maze — no shortcuts, please, and if I got lost, I should simply keep moving until I came across one of the many flags that mark orientation spots.

The corn towered far above my head (come to think of it, even a pro basketball player would have had a hard time seeing over) and the inside walls were so dense that I started to doubt the abilities of my internal compass. I thought of those famous hedge mazes in England when I came to a dead end, and I began to wonder where those orientation flags might be. I took a deep breath, gathered some courage and finished the maze — without resorting to the help of a flag. "Right on," I thought, "I knew I could do it all along."

Now, corn mazes aren't the only things that make Glen Haffy famous. Anyone who fishes knows all about Haffy, and fall colour aficionados always stop at the park on their way to Hockley Valley. And the Bruce Trail marches right through the park on its way north. (Bird lovers should take the trail south out of the park to the area known as The Dingle. A flock of turkeys regularly nests there and the sight is truly incredible.)

The fall colours are, in a word, breathtaking. Lookout Point is located behind the picnic area in the northeast corner of the park and the view is phenomenal. This area is where the roly-poly (and well-forested) Oak Ridges Moraine meets the Niagara Escarpment. I don't think I have to say any more.

Glen Haffy's pièce de résistance is its fishing. I drive by the park on my way to work every day and there's often a line-up of six to eight cars — filled with dedicated anglers — waiting by the gate at eight o'clock (and the park doesn't even open until nine!). Glen Haffy's trout ponds are stocked with the finest rainbow trout I've ever seen. The trout are raised in the Glen Haffy fish hatchery which takes full advantage of its prime location on the cool, clear headwaters of the Humber River.

A helicopter-eye view of the famous corn maze.

*Have you kissed
a trout lately?*

Once again, I was tempted to drop in a line, but I chose to sit back and watch the action instead. A father–son team right in front of me were absorbed in their task at hand, and the young fellow was a quick study. The dad smiled proudly as his junior angler landed his second big fish. I smiled, too. It was just one of those feel-good moments.

I think I'll go back to Glen Haffy for the birding. With its location on the Escarpment and the Oak Ridges Moraine, it is home to the best birds of those very different worlds. (But best of all, my feet will be firmly rooted on the ground.) And since I drive past Glen Haffy every weekday evening, I might even give in and cast a line or two — once I get over the thought of those hooks.

Warbler-mania

Ask any birder about warblers and you'll likely see a flame of excitement light up in their eyes. Birders spend countless hours in spring waiting for a glimpse of these tiny bundles of energy with their flashy colours and distinctive voices. The romance with warblers seems well-founded. These "butterflies of the bird world" like to hide in thick shrubs or treetops where their colourful plumage blends well with the rest of the scenery. If you are lucky to spot a warbler, you'll likely find it difficult to keep it in the focus of your binoculars. They are in constant motion, fluttering from branch to trunk to branch again. The best, and maybe only, time to see a warbler is during spring migration. Each spring, these colourful visitors arrive in waves of a dozen or so at a time. But admire them quickly. These little birds disappear as quickly as they appear.

N O R T H

Baby Bear Pond is the smallest of Tiffin's bears (ponds, that is.)

Tiffin Centre for Conservation

HIGHLIGHTS   Papa Bear, Mama Bear and Baby Bear Ponds Naturalist-led programs available to the public. (Call for information.) Most trails are easily accessible for wheelchairs and strollers. Home of the John L. Jose Environmental Learning Centre, a major education facility for school and community groups. Spring Tonic Maple Syrup Festival.

DIFFICULTY   Beginner

TRAILS   Length: 17 km (Maple Valley, 0.8 km; Hawk Trail, 1.3 km; Rotary Cattail Trail, 1 km; Three Bear Pond Trail, 1 km; Bear Creek Trail, 1.5 km; Beaver Pond Trail, 1.6 km; additional trails, lengths not available).

MARKERS   None, paths are well defined.

SURFACE   Compacted screened gravel, footpaths and some paved access roads.

TYPE   Looped

FACILITIES   Parking, washrooms

OPEN   Year-round access

OWNED AND OPERATED BY
Nottawasaga Valley Conservation Authority

DIRECTIONS   Exit Highway 400 north at Exit 96B, Dunlop Street West, to Angus. Dunlop Street becomes Simcoe Road 90 (formerly Highway 90). From Simcoe Road 90 West, turn left onto Essa Township Concession 8 and travel 4 km south to the signs for the Tiffin Centre.

Wheelchair and Stroller Accessible

Birdwatching

Wildlife Viewing

Fishing

Photography

Maple Syrup

Education Centre

Dogs on Leash Allowed

I used to think that the wind-sculpted white pine trees so master-fully captured on canvas by Canada's own Group of Seven were found only in northern Ontario. Boy, was that perception wrong.

The white pine actually towers above the landscape in many southern Ontario forests, including those found at the Tiffin Centre. This forest giant is quite easy to identify because it doesn't look like any other pine tree. A white pine's trunk is thick and straight, and its elegant canopy sprouts out from the very top of the tree. In some cases, the trunk is actually free of branches for 20 metres or more. This feature has made the white pine the darling of the logging industry, and as a result, there are now as few as ten large stands of old growth white pine left in Ontario. Most of the white pines that you and I will ever see are second growth, and even those are being "harvested."

Tiffin's white pines tower above its newer red pine plantations. Red pine has long been the choice for reforestation because of its ability to withstand even the most

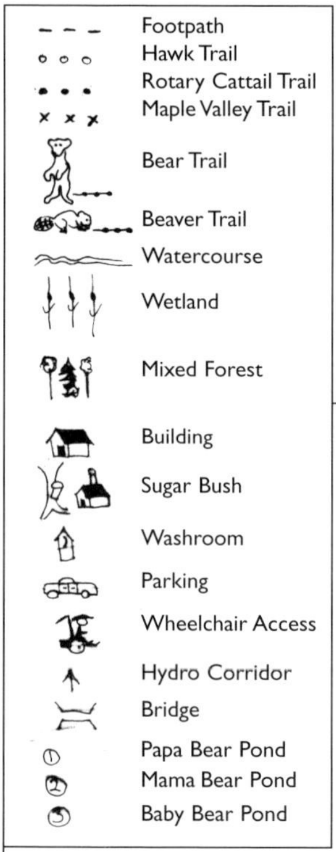

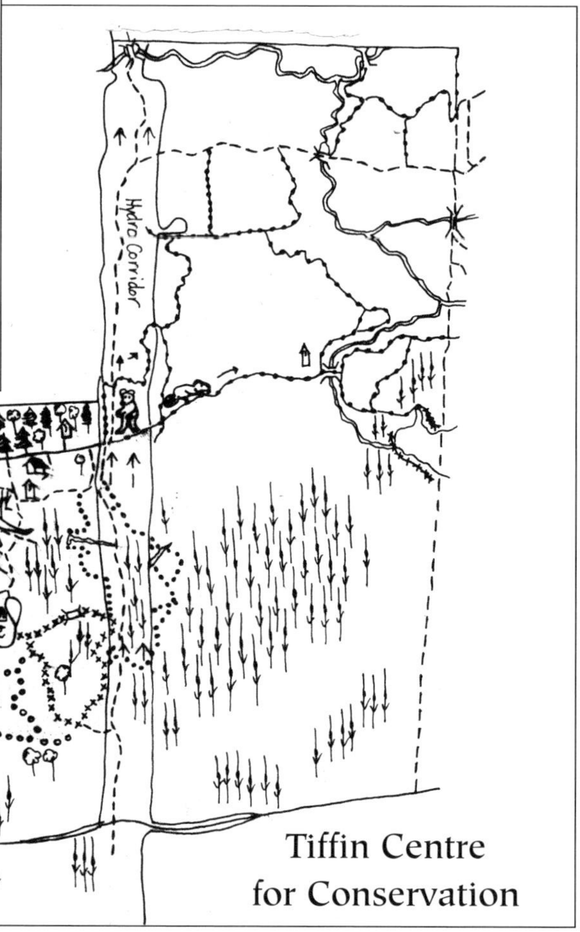

Footpath
Hawk Trail
Rotary Cattail Trail
Maple Valley Trail
Bear Trail
Beaver Trail
Watercourse
Wetland
Mixed Forest
Building
Sugar Bush
Washroom
Parking
Wheelchair Access
Hydro Corridor
Bridge
Papa Bear Pond
Mama Bear Pond
Baby Bear Pond

Hydro Corridor
8th Concession
Essa Township

Tiffin Centre for Conservation

torturous of weather conditions. As I walked through Tiffin's pine plantation, I scanned up and down the branches looking for red crossbills. They're quite at home around pines. The upper and lower parts of a crossbill's beak overlap, giving them the perfect tool for extricating seeds from pine cones. But after quite a bit of aimless wandering I finally realized that the real action in this pine forest wasn't in the trees — it was on the ground.

Beware of flying pine cones whenever you stumble into a red squirrel's territory.

Everywhere I looked, I saw large stacks of green pine cones piled at the bases of trees. At first, I thought this was the work of a couple of busy children but I soon had my senses knocked back into me. As I slowly turned to look up into the trees, I took a pinecone bomb off the old noggin. I know it really shouldn't have hurt all that much, but there's not a lot of flesh on my big forehead. As I rubbed my head, I heard the squeaking laughter of a cantankerous red squirrel. I had clearly stumbled into his winter food storage area and he wanted me out.

Red squirrels are one of the most hyperactive animals I think I have ever seen. They scramble up and down trees at a frantic pace, often launching themselves dangerously through the air to the next tree. They hoard seeds, pine cones and nuts in tree cavities, stumps and virtually any place they think is safe. A single cache of food may contain more than 50 litres of delicacies for the winter and, as I found out, they jealously guard their larders from all potential looters.

This little red squirrel put on quite a show for me. He stomped his feet, jerked his tail and screamed his little head off. This was his territory, not mine. I slowly retreated from his prize pile of cones and left the plantation, but not without the memory — and the bruises — from this pesky leather-jacketed menace.

Feels a little like King Arthur's forest, doesn't it?

Tiffin is definitely a family place. Its trails are generally flat and well maintained, and it offers family-friendly programming that includes environmental camps, a fishing derby, craft shows and a maple syrup festival. It's also home to the Three Bear Pond Trail, which winds its way around — you guessed it — Baby Bear, Mama Bear and Papa Bear ponds. These ponds aren't just for the kids. I spent at least an hour wandering around, snapping pictures for my scrapbook. The fall colours looked as if they were on fire in the late afternoon light, and the reflections on the still water of Papa Bear Pond warranted a full roll of film. My pictures will never be as good as the ones you see in this book, but I had fun anyway. Practice makes perfect, they say.

The Bear Creek and Wetland Trails both make their ways through a hydro corridor, which I have to admit looks really out of place in a conservation area. Thankfully, this unmistakably human part of the landscape has been reclaimed by the local wildlife, which use it as we would use Highway 401. White-tailed deer often travel through this corridor, and eastern screech owls like to perch on the hydro towers to look for their lunch.

Oddly enough, screech owls don't actually screech. These non-migratory, nocturnal beasts aren't all that vocal but when they do speak up, the sound is more like a whinny. (Don't worry, it's not quite like a horse). These tiny owls come in two different colours — red and grey — but you're not likely to see either if you hike only during the day. The only way you'll see a screech during daylight hours is if a cloud of frantic chickadees has led you to the owl's hiding spot. The only screech owl I'd ever seen was one that was part of a rehabilitation program, so I was bound and determined to see one in the wild.

I had read that screech owls can be lured from hiding by imitating their call. I armed myself with a flashlight and set out to the corridor at dusk. The book told me that I should crouch down to lower my silhouette, call out to the owls and then shine my flashlight on them when they inevitably flew in to check me out. I have to say I'm glad there was no one around to see this one. Once again, I'm down on my hands and knees, this time making weird whinnying noises that sounded nothing like they were supposed to. If only my father could have seen me then. "Don't believe everything you read," he would have said. Well, my inability to attract any feathered friends had much more to do with my poor vocal talents than with the instructions from the book, I'm sure. At least I only embarrassed myself in front of the night creatures and my buddy the red squirrel. As I hiked back out to my car, I was almost certain I heard him cackling to himself. And we think we're watching the animals.

How to See Wildlife — Lesson One

Hikers tend to make lots of noise when they're on the trail, giving the local wildlife lots of time to run and hide. If you want to see some wild creatures, you need to slow down and tune in. Instead of galloping along at your usual pace, try slowing down to a tenth of your usual pace. The animals will relax and resume their normal behaviours — and you'll probably see things you never imagined.

Now that you've slowed down, you need to tune in to your surroundings. Walk slowly and softly, and count backwards from 25 to 0. You must concentrate on each number and eliminate all distractions from your mind. Once you're calm and focused, the world will seem a lot bigger than it was just a few minutes before.

Both of these ideas are a lot harder than they seem. With practice and determination, you'll not only see lots of wildlife, but you'll feel better, too.

Fort Willow's palisade and the foundations of all of its buildings
have been reconstructed using archaeological records.

Fort Willow Conservation Area

Birdwatching

Photography

Dogs on Leash Allowed

HIGHLIGHTS   Restored palisade and building foundations of a War of 1812 military fort. Located on the eastern edge of the Minesing Swamp.

DIFFICULTY   Intermediate

TRAIL   Ganaraska Trail
MARKERS   White blazes
SURFACE   Compacted screen gravel
TYPE   Linear

OPEN   Year-round access

OWNED AND OPERATED BY
Nottawasaga Valley Conservation Authority

DIRECTIONS   Exit Highway 400 north at Exit 96B, Dunlop Street West, to Angus. Dunlop Street becomes Simcoe Road 90 (formerly Highway 90). From Simcoe Road 90 West, travel north on Grenfel Road and continue for approximately 5 km to the Fort Willow Conservation Area. The parking area is located on the left side of the road and is well disguised by trees. Watch for a small sign on the right side of the road that indicates the park's location.

The sound of distant gunfire shook me where I stood. At first I thought someone might be using dynamite at some nearby gravel pit, but it was Saturday and there were too many booms for any sane aggregate. Then my thoughts turned to those folks with guns who call themselves "sportspeople." Out of season, thank goodness. I've never had patience for that. Besides, it sounded more like war than anything else.

It took me a few minutes but I soon realized that Fort Willow is only a few kilometres from Canadian Forces Base Borden, a large training base for our country's military. How ironic it felt standing on the site of a British fort from the War of 1812, hearing the volleys of

Nature
HIKES

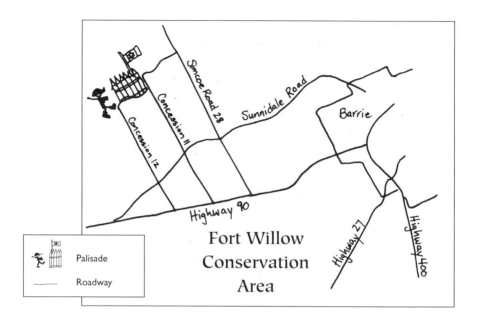

Fort Willow
Conservation
Area

Palisade

Roadway

today's military training manoeuvres in the distance. It was a fitting tribute to an incredible place.

Fort Willow lies on the ancient Nine Mile Portage, one of the three major, early 19th-century gateways to the undeveloped west. This portage route was originally travelled by our country's First Nations people and later used by fur traders of the North West Trading Company. It gained fame during the War of 1812 as the route used by the British to move soldiers and supplies from Lake Simcoe to their ultimate destination at forts on Georgian Bay.

A group of local volunteers called the Fort Willow Improvement Group have used extensive archaeological records to painstakingly reconstruct the fort's palisade and the foundations of all of its buildings. I sat down on a log frame at the back of the fort and was sort of swept away by the sound of the distant guns. Life at the turn of the 19th century would have been difficult enough without purposely choosing to march into the centre of a huge swamp. My boots and I have been calf-deep in the swamp not far from the fort. It wasn't a pretty sight.

The soldiers had constructed a corduroy road to try to make their way through the muck, and I can only imagine how frustrated they must have been. They would have cut down hundreds, maybe thousands, of trees to build a road into a swamp. How futile. My mother grew up near an area not unlike this swamp. She once shared a story about road construction through their wetland (in her case, a somewhat smaller area known as a bog).

Every day, workers would slave from sun-up to sun-down laying cut trees onto the bog to create the road. The next day when they returned, the logs would be gone — sunk deep into the wetland. This frustration would continue for days, even weeks, until there were enough logs under the surface to fill the holes. The workers near my mother's childhood home even lost a bulldozer to the pull of the muck.

I thought of my mother's story as I looked around the Fort. How may soldiers died making that road and the fort, or hauling supplies for the war? How many souls were buried at my feet and how many still lingered around me? I'm not sure if anyone even has the answers to those questions.

Through research, I've learned that Fort Willow and the Nine Mile Portage helped lead the British to victory on the upper Great Lakes. I've also learned that after the war, the Nine Mile Portage was

Fort Willow lies on the ancient Nine Mile Portage.

The cunning red fox patrols the park and nearby swamp.

travelled by some notable explorers, including Sir John Franklin, who travelled through in 1825 on his way to the Arctic, and David Thompson, who returned from his map-making excursion in the new west via the portage.

It's sad to think that my youthful passion for history was snuffed out by one bad teacher. It has taken far too long for me to rekindle my interest — and my respect — for the past. I think I can thank the soldiers at Base Borden for my new-found curiosity. After all, it was their distant training games that triggered my ears — and my imagination.

Fall Colour Photo Tips

Shoot contrasting colours. Look for scenes that contrast the warm reds, oranges and yellows of the fall against cool green and blues. You'll be amazed with the effect.

Increase colour saturation. A polarizing filter produces super-saturated colours (and helps reduce reflections from water and windows, too). Just attach the filter to your 35mm lens and rotate the front section to see the difference!

Bad weather can be good weather. Don't stay inside during those light fall drizzles. The soft, diffused light that accompanies a drizzly day brings out the fine details and subtle colours of fall.

Choose the right film. Fine-grain films (100 ASA print films and 50–100 ASA slide films) always exhibit the richest colours. If you use slide film, try the films often used by the professionals — Fuji Velvia and Kodak 100VS. Comparable print films include Fuji Reala and Kodak Gold.

A spectacular sunrise over Georgian Bay.

Petun Conservation Area

Wildlife Viewing

Birdwatching

Cross-country Skiing

Snowshoeing

Photography

Dogs on Leash Allowed

HIGHLIGHTS   Rugged and wild with spectacular views to Georgian Bay. Located on Niagara Escarpment. Bruce Trail winds through the park.

DIFFICULTY   Advanced

TRAIL MARKERS   Bruce Trail
White blazes for main trail; blue or yellow for side trails.

SURFACE   Rugged footpaths

TYPE   Linear

OPEN   Year-round access

OWNED AND OPERATED BY
Nottawasaga Valley Conservation Authority

DIRECTIONS   From Collingwood, travel southwest on Grey County Road 19 (it's at the west end of town) until it turns sharply to the west on a section called New Mountain Road. Turn left onto Concession 2 and travel south to the park. Bruce Trail parking is located up the hill beyond the park's gate. This section of Concession 2 may be dangerous during winter. Please park on road near the park gate (take care not to block the Petun gate or the farmer's gate adjacent to it), and hike up the road and around the corner at the top of the hill to the Bruce Trail.

The sound of a bird hitting a window is sickening. I wasn't more than a few hundred metres inside the closed gate at Petun when a small group of cedar waxwings flew by me. They were playing and cavorting in mid-air, and as they flew past the small building visible from the road, all of the birds flew up and over the building's roof — all except one.

I ran over to the limp mass of feathers and carefully scooped it up into my hands. I tried to revive the beautiful masked creature with the CPR techniques a good friend had taught me. I gently rubbed its chest to stimulate its heart and repeatedly extended its wings in an attempt

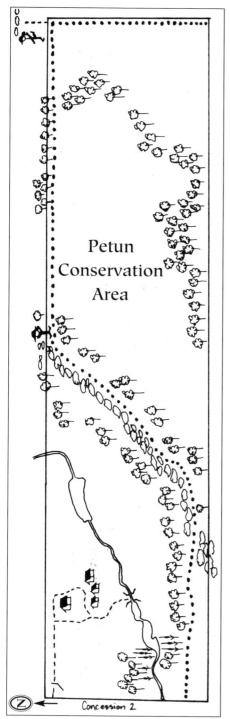

Petun
Conservation
Area

Concession 2

to force air into its tiny lungs. As a tear slipped down my cheek, I realized that my efforts had been in vain. Its delicate neck was broken from the impact and it had likely died instantly.

Cedar waxwings are polite, easy-going birds that tolerate relatively close contact with humans. They often perch together on tree branches, gingerly passing berries and fruit down the line to each other. Their black masks, red wingtips and a distinctive yellow bar across the tips of their tails make the waxwing an easy spot for amateur birders. My only solace in the bird's untimely demise was that it was late May and the bird was unlikely to have had a mate. A few weeks later and the loss would have been far more acute. A death then would have left a female waxwing stranded, without food, on a clutch of eggs. I didn't even want to think about that.

After my experience with the injured bird, I left Petun for the day. I just didn't have the heart to go for a hike. I took the little fellow home with me and buried it in my yard. I even created a small stone cairn to mark the

• • •	Bruce Trail	🏠	Building
- - -	Petun Trail	↟↟↟	Wetland / Swamp
∿	Watercourse	⌒	Niagara Escarpment
⋈	Bridge	🏃	Happy Hiker
🌳🌳🌳	Forest Cover	)	Locked Gate

There's no better place to take in the view.

grave. I know it sounds so awfully human but I thought it was the least I could do.

My experience aside, Petun is an extraordinarily beautiful place in every season. The Bruce Trail passes through the park and from its vantage point high on the Escarpment, you can see Georgian Bay in all its splendour. Access to the Bruce Trail is a bit unorthodox (you can't actually get to it from the main park entrance) but it's well worth the search. In summer, you can drive past the park entrance, up the hill and around the curve at the top to find the Bruce Trail parking. I wouldn't advise a winter car trip up the hill unless you have a four-wheeler, and even then, you might be wise to leave your car by the gate and walk. Just be sure to park away from the Petun gate and the farm gate immediately adjacent to the park.

The Bruce Trail hike through the park is spectacular. The terrain is extremely rugged and well suited to those with some adventurous blood in their veins. I took to the trail after a freak early November snowstorm that left almost 30 cm of the white stuff on the ground. Of course, it hadn't even dawned on me that I should take my snowshoes so I spent the better part of an afternoon slipping and sliding around

The ghosts of the forest hide the secrets of the past.

on snow-covered rocks. I could see why this part of the trail was a favourite of extreme cross-country skiers.

The park takes its name from the Petun, a band of First Nations people who lived in the area in the 1500s and 1600s. The Petun farmed the slopes of the Niagara Escarpment from Creemore to Craigleith but were destroyed by the neighbouring Seneca Nation after a devastating outbreak of smallpox weakened their tribe. An ancient Petun village has been unearthed north of the park boundaries at Bruce Trail km 51.2. (Check a Bruce Trail Guide for directions.)

Slowed by snow and and concerned about the setting sun, I didn't make it all the way to the ancient village, but that didn't seem to matter much. The wind through the woods seemed to carry some mysterious presence that walked with me on my journey. Whether you believe in spirituality or religion or perhaps just in some kind of higher power, Petun certainly has it. You just need to slow down and open yourself to the possibility.

I stood on the lookout on the edge of the Escarpment and gazed northwest toward Georgian Bay. I tucked my chin inside my coat as the cold wind stung my face. Below me, the Bruce–Petun Side Trail descended through some massive limestone blocks to the forest floor below. Beside me, a small white cedar had wrapped its bare, arthritic roots around a rock. I put my hand on the tree's trunk and suddenly felt very small. This cedar could easily be over a thousand years old. My presence on this earth would be but a blink in time to this tree. The things it has seen!

Humans are not easily humbled by nature — unless we allow ourselves to be. We never let down our guard long enough to really feel nature. We keep it at I gazed length, denying the possibility that everything around us — the grasses, the trees, the birds, the rocks, the mammals — all have some sentient quality to them.

I whispered a quiet thank you to the tree before I walked away, and vowed that I'd remember this moment whenever I felt a swell of arrogance rising in my chest. I'm one very tiny piece of a much larger puzzle and I can never forget that. Petun won't let me.

Courting the Birds

Birds demonstrate a wide variety of courtship behaviours to attract a mate. If you're lucky, you may see some of these springtime antics.

Male blue jays, house sparrows and grackles tilt their heads and bodies as if they were bowing to their queens. Hummingbirds, larks and buntings embark on a dramatic courtship flight, rising high into the sky and singing loudly, in their attempts to attract mates. Ovenbirds, kinglets and eastern kingbirds are a little more subtle with their affections. These males raise their head feathers to display a brightly coloured patch.

Robins, orioles and tanagers parade around their betrothed, strutting to show off their most colourful feathers. Woodpeckers are in a class all their own. They spread and close their wing and tail feathers to show off their bright plumage and use their beaks to drum on anything they can find, including steel drums and buildings. Pigeons, doves, flickers and crows are quite different — courtship involves both partners. The male and female face each other and dip their heads quickly and repeatedly to declare their intent.

Water lilies blanket the Mad River as it passes through the wetlands.

Leopard frogs keep a low profile in the reeds.

Osprey Wetlands

Canoeing

Birdwatching

Wildlife Viewing

Birdwatching

Fishing

Photography

Dogs on Leash Allowed

HIGHLIGHTS   Wild and wonderful.
Great birding from the adjacent roadways.
Perfect habitat for brook trout.
Orchids, orchids, orchids.

DIFFICULTY   Advanced

TRAIL   Unknown

OPEN   Year-round access

OWNED BY   Nottawasaga Valley Conservation Authority

DIRECTIONS   Travel north on Highway 24 from Shelburne. The south end of the park is located on Durham Road, west of Highway 24. To access the north end of the wetlands, continue on to Osprey Township Concession 2. Turn left and the bridge will soon appear.

The Web is a pretty incredible tool. Sure it's fun (I've even searched my own name to see if I cyber-exist) but the thing I love most about the Web is the wealth of information I now have at my fingertips. I can just sit and soak it up like a giant sponge. You might wonder how the World Wide Web could possibly relate to this story about Osprey Wetlands, a marshy area near the head of the Mad River? Let me tell you.

It all started with some research I was doing on endangered and vulnerable species. Like most people on-line, I couldn't resist the temptation to do a search on the area that I actually live in (admit it, you've done it, too). I was searching the on-line version of the *Ontario Atlas Map of Birds* for birds of prey and somehow clicked on Least Bittern.

Least Bitterns are acrobatic little herons that can camouflage themselves in reeds and cattails so well that you might be only a few metres away from one and never know it. They're a bit weird — they'd rather run away and hide than fly to safety — but maybe that's what makes them so interesting. When the atlas map came up, I discovered that this nationally vulnerable species might be nesting near the area of

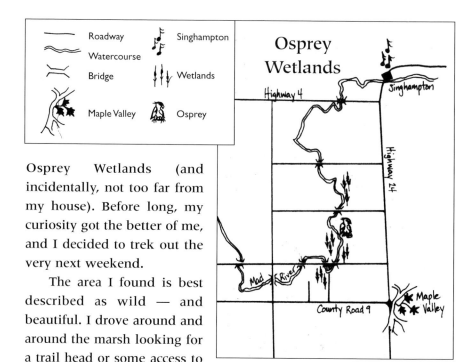

Osprey Wetlands (and incidentally, not too far from my house). Before long, my curiosity got the better of me, and I decided to trek out the very next weekend.

The area I found is best described as wild — and beautiful. I drove around and around the marsh looking for a trail head or some access to the park, but I didn't find anything. I finally resorted to simply pulling off to the side of Concession 2 and standing on the bridge with my binoculars. I had to laugh when I saw the tell tale sign of a good fishing hole — three or four lures were dangling from the overhanging hydro lines. No wonder the big ones always get away.

I had only been on that bridge for five or ten minutes when I spotted some movement out the corner of my eye. I turned my head just in time to see the distinctive crooked wings and black mask of — you guessed it — an osprey. I had come up empty-handed in my search for osprey at Island Lake, and there I was at Osprey Wetlands looking for something else entirely when one almost dropped in my lap. And to think I actually thought the name of the wetlands came from the township name.

I gave chase (a word to the wise — don't ever try to run while looking through binoculars) and my big black lab, my faithful outdoor companion, decided to chase me. I'm sure she thought it was a game, just like the one where she takes my legs out from under me whenever I run to answer the phone.

The elusive least bittern clings to a reed as it hunts for its dinner.

As I lay at the edge of the road picking little bits of gravel out of my mouth, I thought long and hard about whether a woman is really safer in the woods with a dog or without. And as I looked toward the edge of the wetland, I could have sworn I saw a black and brown blur at the base of some cattails. All I could do was laugh. I decided there were a whole lot of things I'd do differently the next time I went back to Osprey Wetlands. Next time, I'm going in — and the dog will be staying home to surf the 'Net.

Plant Invaders

So what's the big deal about non-native plants? Sure, they look pretty and most are relatively benign, but some are aggressive invaders that spread rapidly to change the nature — and health — of our ecosystems. As many as 40% of the wild plants found in southern Ontario are non-native exotic species.

Purple loosestrife was originally introduced to gardeners as a colourful ornamental flower, but it soon escaped human control and now chokes wetlands across the eastern part of North America. Native plants cannot compete with its invasive root system and soon die out.

Garlic mustard can produce as many as 100,000 seeds per square metre of soil and can take over an entire forest floor in only a few years. Native wildflowers and tree seedlings are strangled by this plant, leaving the forest unable to regenerate.

Other dangerous exotic species include Norway maple, Canada thistle, dog-strangling vine, common buckthorn and reed canary grass. Your local Conservation Authority works to control and remove these dangerous plants, and to maintain strong native habitats for all living things.

The Ganaraska Trail offers beautiful views of the swamp.

One of the best ways to see the swamp is on a tour with the Friends of Minesing Swamp. Pied piper Harold McMaster stands second from the left.

Minesing Swamp

Canoeing

Wildlife Viewing

Birdwatching

Fishing

Photography

Dogs on Leash Allowed

HIGHLIGHTS Internationally significant Ramsar Convention wetland. Home to Ontario's fifth largest and oldest Great Blue Heron colonies. Eastern edges home to large number of winter deer yards and a stunning vista. Home to string fens, large pure silver maple stands and beautiful orchid beds.

DIFFICULTY   Intermediate to Difficult

TRAIL   Ganaraska Trail
MARKERS   White blazes
SURFACE   Compacted screen gravel
TYPE   Linear

OPEN   Year-round access

OWNED AND MANAGED BY
Nottawasaga Valley Conservation Authority

DIRECTIONS   **Via the Nottawasaga River Canoe Route:**
See the section devoted specifically to the canoe route for directions to its many access points.

Via the Ganaraska Trail:
The Ganaraska Trail skirts the southern perimeter of Minesing Swamp. You can access it easily at:
EAST SIDE — Exit Highway 400 north at Exit 96B, Dunlop Street West, to Angus. Dunlop Street becomes Simcoe Road 90 (formerly Highway 90). From Simcoe Road 90 West, travel north on Grenfel Road to the Fort Willow Conservation Area. You can access the Ganaraska Trail from the back of the Fort Willow palisade.
WEST SIDE — The Ganaraska Trail Club advises that this part of their trail is now closed. It is still used extensively by hikers and hunters but it is an extremely wet trail during rainy seasons with lots and lots of bugs. If you want to explore this section during dry seasons or in winter, follow these instructions: from Simcoe Road 90 West (formerly Highway 90), travel north on the 22nd Sideroad. This is a dead-end road. A large Minesing Swamp sign marks the entrance.

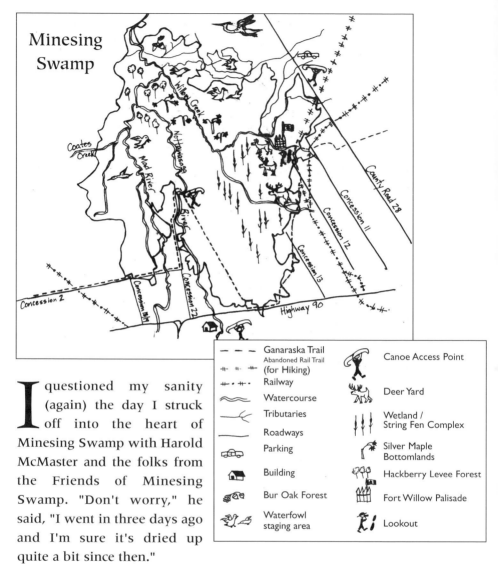

Minesing Swamp

– – – Ganaraska Trail	Canoe Access Point
₊₊ ₊₊ ₊₊ Abandoned Rail Trail (for Hiking)	
₊₊ ₊ ₊₊ Railway	Deer Yard
～ Watercourse	
⌇ Tributaries	Wetland / String Fen Complex
— Roadways	
🚗 Parking	Silver Maple Bottomlands
🏠 Building	Hackberry Levee Forest
🐦 Bur Oak Forest	Fort Willow Palisade
🦢 Waterfowl staging area	Lookout

I questioned my sanity (again) the day I struck off into the heart of Minesing Swamp with Harold McMaster and the folks from the Friends of Minesing Swamp. "Don't worry," he said, "I went in three days ago and I'm sure it's dried up quite a bit since then."

I had visited the edges of the swamp many times before but this was the first time I was able to explore its inner reaches. Water in one form or another is never far away in this more than 6000-hectare sponge, and my recently waterproofed boots were about to face the biggest test of their career.

The only really safe way to go off-trail exploring in this magnificent wetland is with a well-seasoned guide. The McMaster family has owned land in the Swamp since the 1920s so I put my trust (and the fate of my boots) in Harold's able hands. He assured us that the best way to travel inland was via an animal highway, specifically a deer trail. We nodded with anticipation and followed our pied piper into the swamp.

Minesing is a patchwork quilt of private and public lands that are home to a phenomenal number of plants, birds, mammals, reptiles, amphibians and fish, including Ontario's fifth largest (and oldest) blue heron colony; a huge number of deer yards (where deer spend their winters); and blanket after blanket of rare orchid beds. It's also a complex network of swamps, marshes, bogs and string fens, which are easy to confuse until you actually stick your foot into one.

It didn't take me long to discover the soggy difference between a string fen and a swamp. A string fen is a very poorly drained area with sedges, grasses and reeds that can usually be visually identified at some distance. A swamp, on the other hand, is a wooded area where shallow water occurs seasonally or persists for long periods of time. In a swamp, the ground can be stable one step and wet the next. Needless to say my boots were done for.

Our first thrill came when a member of our group spotted a large porcupine slumbering in the bough of a wind-worn white pine. Contrary to popular belief, porcupines cannot throw their quills. A porcupine will turn its back on its predator, bristle its quills and swing its tail. Once contact is made, the quills pull loose from the tail and impale their then miserable opponent. The quills will migrate into the victim's body and can be fatal if they find their way through a major organ. With that tidbit of knowledge, we continued down the trail, agreeing that porcupines look much better asleep than wide awake.

Our hopes were high that we might catch a glimpse of a white-tailed deer, one of Minesing's most common mammals. Well, we may have been travelling on one of their many highways, but they certainly weren't. The thunderous steps of more than a dozen over-eager animal detectives kept even the effervescent black-capped chickadees away.

Deer trails are quite easy to recognize if you know what to look for. The vegetation around the well-used trail will be worn or matted and the soil may actually be grooved to take on a U-shape. Deer trails connect significant bedding, feeding and watering areas, and often have a number of smaller, less frequently used paths called runs branching away from them. Our trail took us directly to the winding waters of Willow Creek and then to a lush cedar grove that is home to a major deer yard each winter.

Of course, Minesing Swamp is home to more than just porcupine and white-tailed deer. This special place provides habitat to no fewer than 400 different plant species, including a number that are classified as provincially rare, and close to 225 kinds of birds, including 135 nesting varieties. Twenty-three types of mammals, 30 kinds of fish and a number of reptiles and amphibians also roam Minesing's vast network of wetlands. Claims that black bear have occasionally lived in the swamp were confirmed by a reputable source — our hike leader, Harold McMaster.

Harold's eyes saddened as he recounted the memory of the two orphaned black bear cubs his family desperately tried to hand-raise. They were adopted on January 27, 1951, after the mother bear had been accidentally killed while she lay hibernating in her den. Harold and his father took the hairless, one-week-old cubs home, and the members of their family all took turns feeding them with an eyedropper. One cub died three weeks after being rescued, but the other one thrived, gaining an incredible 30 pounds by June. Soon, the energetic bear became too much for the McMasters to handle and the Bowmanville Zoo agreed to give it a temporary home. The McMasters believe that the cub eventually lived a long and happy life in a New York State zoo.

Rest assured that black bear sightings in Minesing are extremely rare, so you probably won't need that bear bell you've always wanted to buy. You will need a good compass, though, and you'd better know how to use it, particularly in spring. In spring, canoeists head into the swamp via the Nottawasaga River Canoe Route, but flooding can make the river virtually indistinguishable from those wetlands, fens, marshes and bogs I described earlier. Canoeing may keep your feet dry, but you just might stray from the river and find yourself lost. (More about the canoe route in the next chapter.)

In 1996, Minesing Swamp received international recognition from the Ramsar Convention on Wetlands for its environmental diversity and importance. This special designation gives it the same stature as better-known wetlands like the Baltic Marshes and the famous Florida Everglades. And while it certainly doesn't have any alligators,

Minesing does have its own roster of uniquely courageous creatures. Harold shared an experience with us that he can still barely believe himself. He enthusiastically showed us a small pool of water beneath a culvert where he had recently found a small fish. A fish swimming around in a pool didn't seem all that remarkable to us until we tracked the creature's remarkable journey. That fish had travelled what seemed like hundreds of metres through nothing more than a slow trickle of water and dense vegetation. Its perseverance astounded us and reinforced that where there is a will, there is a way.

Minesing Swamp is an extraordinary jewel in the Conservation Journeys crown. Each time you visit, you'll discover a new and equally remarkable piece of its character. Visit often and if you ever get a chance to explore with Harold and his band of merry Friends, do it. The insights and memories of these sage folks are as unique as the swamp itself. Listen carefully — you won't be disappointed.

Wonderful Wetlands

S wamps, fens, marshes and bogs play important roles in the health of our ecosystems. They provide critical food, water, shelter and space for fish, wildlife, birds and insects, including more than one-third of North America's endangered species, and they help prevent flooding and erosion. Wetlands also act like giant filters, trapping and removing pollutants and sediment that are washed off nearby land.

Wetlands have long been drained, dredged and filled for agriculture or development. Minesing Swamp has not escaped these pressures. In the early 1900s, a number of drainage ditches were dug to create farmland and improve spring drainage. Instead, these ditches left some areas of the swamp permanently flooded, killing important forest lands and disrupting delicate wildlife habitats.

Today, those activities have ceased, thanks in part to the efforts of the Nottawasaga Valley Conservation Authority. They work with governments, land owners and other local groups to actively protect and manage this wonderful wetland.

Neither rain, sleet nor snow can keep a paddler down! Those crazy Friends of the Minnesing Swamp will paddle in any kind of weather.

Nottawasaga River Canoe Route

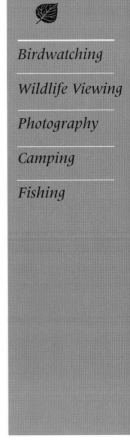

Birdwatching

Wildlife Viewing

Photography

Camping

Fishing

HIGHLIGHTS   One of the longest navigable river routes in southern Ontario Best way to see the internationally significant Minesing Swamp.

DIFFICULTY   Intermediate

ROUTE   Length: 80 km
MARKERS   Red slashes on trees
SURFACE   Water
TYPE   Linear

FACILITIES   Two canoe campsites

MANAGED BY Nottawasaga Valley Conservation Authority

DIRECTIONS   There are five access points to the
                 Canoe Route:

Nicolston Dam: Take Highway 89 west to Nicolston Dam, east of Alliston. Go north on Essa Township Concession 5. Look for the brown canoe access symbol at the iron bridge.

Essa Centennial Park: From Highway 89 take Concession 6 north to Sideroad 20 and go west. Camping ($5) is not permitted at this site, but only if you arrive by canoe.

Nottawasaga Valley Conservation Authority Office: Take Highway 400 north, exit at Exit 96B and travel west on Simcoe County Road 90 toward Angus. Watch for signs.

Edenvale Conservation Area: Take Highway 400 north, exit at Exit 96B and travel west on Simcoe Road 90 toward Angus. Turn north onto Simcoe Country Road 28 and then west on Highway 26. The park is on your right. Canoe camping is permitted at this site.

Schooner Parkette: Take Highway 400 north, exit at Bayfield Street (Exit 98) and travel northwest on Highway 26 to Elmvale. In Elmvale, turn west on Highway 92, which becomes River Road. The Parkette is located in Wasaga Beach, on the south side of River Road before the bridge.

The Nottawasaga Valley Conservation Authority recommends that canoeists leave the river at Schooner Parkette. The area of the river between the parkette and Georgian Bay is heavily used by motor boats and water skiers.

CAUTIONS

- Be careful in early spring, as cold water, high water levels, strong currents and floating debris make canoeing extremely dangerous.

- Watch for deadheads (partially submerged logs).

- Beware of the rapids; they are relatively small but may represent a hazard for novice canoeists.

- Do not stray from the river channel in Minesing Swamp, especially during high water levels. You could get lost.

- Carry plenty of insect repellent, particularly in May and June.

- Watch for stinging nettle and poison ivy if you portage in Minesing Swamp.

SPECIAL   Nottawasaga Valley Conservation Authority hosts an annual Minesing in the Spring interpretive canoe tour on the last weekend of May every year. Contact the Conservation Authority for more information

---

Have I mentioned yet that I can't swim? A bad childhood swimming lesson experience with three power-hungry teenage instructors (Yes, I'm still bitter — I can even remember their names) drained any enthusiasm I had for the water out of my tiny frame. I did eventually learn how to swim at an athletic camp but a bad knee injury kept me from earning anything more than the lowly yellow badge (stop laughing).

So, I can hear you asking yourself: What could such a landlubber ever tell me about a canoe route? Easy! Once I don a life jacket, I'm as confident in water as a dolphin (although not nearly as graceful). I have whitewater rafted in a tiny four-person raft with some crazy friends who wanted to show me the skills they had picked up along the Colorado River. I have rowed along the edge of Long Island Sound in search of crabs. I have sea-kayaked on the St. Lawrence River in the middle of a pod of beluga whales. And I have dipped my beautiful cherry otter tail paddle into the Nottawasaga River.

The Nottawasaga Canoe Route is a 75 km paddle from the Nicolston Dam, just east of Alliston, to Wasaga Beach, the largest freshwater beach in the world. The route is divided into three parts: the 32.5 km southern section from Nicolston to Angus; the 19 km Minesing Swamp section; and the 23.5 km northern section from Edenvale to Wasaga Beach.

Shoreline

Canoe Access

Portage

Nottawasaga Valley
Conservation Authority Offfice

Canoe Camping Only

Minesing Swamp

Watercourse
Tributary

Nottawasaga River
Canoe Route

NOTTAWASAGA
BAY
Wasaga Beach

Schooner
Parkette
Marl
Lake

Jacks
Lake

Nottawasaga River

Highway 26

County Road 10

Edenvale
Conservation
Area

Sideroad 21/42

Highway 90

Angus

Pine River

Essa Centennial
Park

Sideroad 20

Sideroad 15

Nottawasaga

Sideroad 5

Boyne
River

Highway 89

The southern leg is generally a quiet paddle through pastoral farmland, but there are a few rapids in the gorge near Essa Centennial Park that will give your heart a little rush if the water level is right. The middle section is the best, and probably the only, way to see the ecological treasures hidden deep in Minesing Swamp. It's also a confusing and dangerous paddle in spring when the water swells well over the river banks. The northern leg features small rapids, Jack's Lake and some incredibly beautiful parabolic sand dunes. Ambitious paddlers who want to explore the route's entire length can set up camp at sites in Angus and Edenvale.

Well, I may be confident but I'm not crazy. The thought of heading off into Minesing Swamp in the middle of a spring flood just didn't appeal to me. I have a lot to learn about top maps and compasses and there are probably dozens of better places for me to learn. Fall is my favourite season and the water levels then are low but navigable, so I struck off with a friend for a September paddle.

*Tip your paddle to the anglers
who line the shore.*

The concession roads near the Angus access were lined with cars and I naively thought they all belonged to canoeists. Was I ever wrong. The river banks were packed, virtually shoulder-to-shoulder, with anglers intent on landing the salmon who were making their way inland to spawn. We continued on to Sideroad 21/22 and drove as far into the Swamp as we could. We launched the canoe at the iron bridge that marks the end of the concession and we paddled north to distance ourselves from the anglers.

September is a great time to paddle because the skies are virtually bug free. (Just keep an eye out for low water levels.) The sun warmed us as we paddled, and we glimpsed the first hints of the spectacular kaleidoscope of fall colour still to come. Huge salmon passed beside the canoe and soon the only sounds we heard were the delicate songs of the birds and the rhythms of our paddles slicing the water. This was, and is, the life. My first trip on the Nottawasaga was short and sweet, but it certainly won't be my last. And once this non-swimmer learns some map skills, who knows what might come?

No words needed.

The Canoeist's Craft

Beginners shouldn't worry about having perfect paddle strokes — there are other, more important skills (and things) to focus on.

1. Make sure your personal flotation device (PFD) fits properly and do not be tempted to sit on it instead of wearing it.

2. Know how to swim.

3. Paddle with an experienced friend who can teach you the basics of canoeing.

4. Make sure you can get in and out of a canoe without dumping as the canoe drifts away from the dock or shore.

5. Learn to brace and get comfortable with your balance to handle unexpected winds or motorboat wakes.

6. Learn enough stokes to paddle efficiently and practise paddling without hitting the side of the canoe.

7. Perfect your paddling on the opposite side to your partner. This is the best way to learn and the method you'll use 95% of the time you're on the water.

At the edge of Freedom Rock.

Nottawasaga Bluffs Conservation Area

Wildlife Viewing

Birdwatching

Photography

Dogs on Leash Allowed

HIGHLIGHTS   Awesome cliffs, crevices and caves Old-growth white cedar forest. Isolated natural environment located on the Niagara Escarpment.

DIFFICULTY   Advanced

TRAIL MARKERS	Bruce Trail
	White for main trail; yellow or blue for side trails.
SURFACE	Footpath
TYPE	Linear with some loops.

GANARASKA TRAIL

MARKERS	White blazes
SURFACE	Compacted screen gravel
TYPE	Linear
FACILITIES	Parking
OPEN	Year-round access

OWNED AND OPERATED BY
Nottawasaga Valley Conservation Authority

DIRECTIONS   This park is hard to find, but the search is well worth the effort. Follow Highway 24 north from Shelburne to the hamlet of Singhampton. Turn south at Milltown Road and then east on Ewing Road. Follow the gravel road as it twists and turns toward the park. The parking lot is located at the junction of Concession 10 and the 15/16 Sideroad. There is a small sign that marks the parking lot.

ALTERNATE ROUTE FOR FOUR-WHEEL DRIVE ACCESS ONLY
In Glen Huron, travel south along County Road 62. As you make your way up the hill, you will come to a narrow dirt road (Sideroad 15/16) on your right. Since this sideroad is not cared for between Glen Huron and the Nottawasaga Bluffs parking lot, it is best not to drive it unless you have a vehicle with high ground clearance. The road is strewn with rocks and furrowed from the erosive force of rain storms. In some places, it tracks extremely close to the cliff's edge. If you choose to take this road, please drive slowly and be prepared to negotiate with any oncoming vehicles for safe right-of-way.

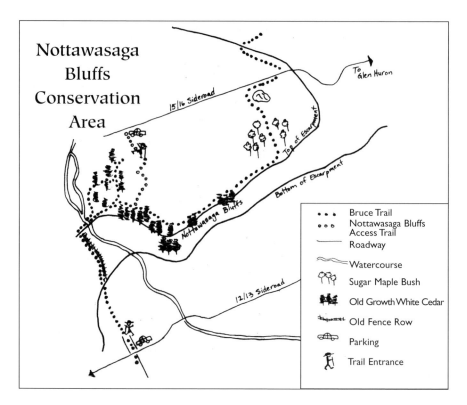

Nottawasaga
Bluffs
Conservation
Area

To Glen Huron

15/16 Sideroad

Top of Escarpment

Bottom of Escarpment

Nottawasaga Bluffs

12/13 Sideroad

• • •	Bruce Trail
○ ○ ○	Nottawasaga Bluffs Access Trail
——	Roadway
≈≈≈	Watercourse
🌳🌳	Sugar Maple Bush
🌲🌲	Old Growth White Cedar
┼┼┼	Old Fence Row
🚗	Parking
🚶	Trail Entrance

T he Bluffs has to be my favourite location in this entire book. I've thought long and hard about why that is, but it's hard to put the emotions into words. I guess the smile that creeps across my face whenever I talk about it says it all.

My resolve to explore this wild place was set when a regular Bluffs hiker asked, "You do have a four-wheel-drive truck, right?" I didn't know quite what to expect that first time I set out to visit the Bluffs but my sense of adventure had been stirred. Sometimes you just have to go for it.

The back way in from Glen Huron is incredibly beautiful and more than just a little rocky. The truck was handy but don't worry — there's another way to get to the Bluffs that's accessible to even the tiniest of cars. Being strong-willed (at least that's what my mother would call it), I took the challenging route in.

As the truck rumbled along the unassumed roadway, a beautiful osprey soared overhead. What a sight. Hawks and eagles have always been strong totems for me, so I took it as a sign of even greater things to come.

The sign marking the Nottawasaga Bluffs Access Trail is relatively small and quite easy to miss if you're travelling fast. The trail itself tracks through what appears to be an old farm field, into a hardwood forest, and then emerges into a narrow band of cedars. As I emerged through the trees the rush of adrenaline that swept over me told me my trek had been well worth the effort. The vista was breathtaking and the drop was, in a word, steep.

I stood near the edge of Freedom Rock Lookout and took it all in. The sights and the sounds of this wild place were so different from the noise of the city that it took me a few minutes to tune my senses to the commotion around me. I suddenly became aware of a beautiful, almost lyrical birdsong. I scanned the forest canopy below — yes, below — for the singer. I caught a glimpse of the crimson breast of this whistling, warbling wonder and quickly realized that I had just seen my first ever rose-breasted grosbeak. Grosbeaks are big eaters and this fellow was no exception. He flew from tree to tree, singing between billfuls of insects and deciduous seeds.

As I trained my binoculars on the bird, I saw more than I had bargained for. Directly ahead of me in a tall pine tree sat a hungry porcupine. He didn't seem to care much about me — dinner was far more important. He very quietly munched on the tree, leaving a large scar in the bark. A quick glance around me revealed the extent of his destruction. A number of trees had large bare patches on their trunks and many were scarred around their complete circumference. A tree's bark transports critical nutrients from the roots to the leaves and once it has been pierced around the trunk, the tree dies. Sadly, a number of nearby trees showed various stages of decline.

Nottawasaga Bluffs lies on the Niagara Escarpment, a UNESCO World Biosphere Reserve. World Biosphere Reserves are unique areas that have successfully balanced the preservation of significant ecosystems with the pressures of surrounding development. This designation places the Escarpment in the company of internationally renowned areas like the Florida Everglades, the Serengeti Desert and the Galapagos Islands.

Nowhere is the dramatic landscape of the Escarpment more evident than at the Bluffs. Rugged cliffs thrust high into the sky, sharp crevices drop deep into darkness and the gnarled roots of an old-

Take pictures during the golden hours of light —
just after dawn and just before dusk. Scenes that look ordinary at noon
become extraordinary in the right light.

growth white cedar forest cling to the rocks along this ancient land-form. That's right — Nottawasaga Bluffs is home to white cedar trees that are well over 1000 years old.

Now, when I think of old-growth forest, I picture massive trees that take at least three people to wrap their arms all the way around. This old-growth forest is different. These white cedars seem to grow right out of the rock face and their wind torn, gnarled roots lie exposed to all extremes of weather. Faced with such severe conditions, the trees here grow so slowly that a 10 cm tall "seedling" could actually be more than 50 years old. Yes, you read it right — 50 years old.

Under normal conditions, a white cedar would likely have about 12 growth rings (one per year) for every 2.5 cm of diameter. The cedars at the Bluffs and along the Escarpment have more than 200 growth rings for every 2.5 cm of diameter. Each ring is smaller than a human hair.

The oldest living tree found along the Escarpment is more than 1650 years old, and the dead trees I saw as I hiked along the Bruce

Trail section of the park might actually have lived a few thousand years ago. As I rested my hand on the trunk of a 1000-year-old tree, a black and white warbler scooted onto a nearby branch. In that moment, I wondered how many other warblers or porcupines or grosbeaks had ever rested on that same branch — and how many more would pause there over the next 1000 years. Right then and there, I realized just how small one person could be.

I guess you could say this place moved me. I've now been back to the Bluffs in every season, scrambled up and down its many rocks and crevices, posed on its edge for way too many photos (yes, that's me on the cover of the book) and pondered the musings of a local farmer that are carved into the dolomite rock of the cliffs. Every visit shows me something new, but that first adventure has remained the most vivid in my mind. As I turned to walk back to the truck that day, a long dark shadow running through the hardwoods stopped me dead in my tracks. My senses were so alive that I actually felt a rush of panic. It was too fast for a porcupine, too long for a raccoon and hopefully too small for a black bear. Once my heart stopped racing, I realized that I had likely just seen a fisher, an elusive and somewhat rare mammal

Yellow spotted salamanders hide in the park's many rocks and crevices.

that counts porcupine as its number-one delicacy. It was probably startled as much by me as I was by it. It took a few minutes for me to pull myself together, but scare or no scare, I knew I'd be back. This place was unforgettable.

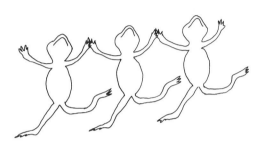

The Bruce Trail

This famous 1000-km foot path winds its way along the Niagara Escarpment from Queenston, near Niagara Falls, to Fathom Five Provincial Park in Tobermory. You will find its trademark white blazes on trees, rocks and fence posts in six of the places featured in this book: the Nottawasaga Bluffs, Terra Cotta, Glen Haffy, Belfountain, Albion Hills and Petun Conservation Areas.

The vision for this extraordinary trail was conceived in 1959 as a way to stir public support to protect the unique ecology of the Escarpment. More than 300 species of birds, 53 types of mammals, 35 varieties of reptiles and amphibians, 90 fish species and a number of insects make their home on the this remarkable landform. The trail itself is part of an important greenway that acts as a migratory corridor for thousands of birds, animals, reptiles and amphibians, including a number of rare and endangered species.

S O U T H

Jet streams from passing planes cut the crisp morning air.

An eastern kingbird belts out a favourite tune.

Rattray Marsh Conservation Area

HIGHLIGHTS Last shingle bar wetland in the region. Spectacular view of CN Tower and Toronto skyline. Birdwatcher's paradise. Lots of quiet spots to sit and watch the world go by.

DIFFICULTY Novice

TRAILS Length: 3.5 km
MARKERS None
SURFACE Boardwalks and footpaths are clearly visible.
TYPE Looped

IMPORTANT The plant and animal communities in the Marsh are extremely sensitive. Please stay on the designated trails to minimize harm to the fragile environment.

LINKS TO Waterfront Trail

OPEN: Year-round access

OWNED AND OPERATED BY
Credit Valley Conservation Authority

DIRECTIONS The main entrance to Rattray Marsh is through Jack Darling Park on Lakeshore Road West (Highway 2) between Port Credit and Clarkson in the City of Mississauga. This entrance includes a bridge with steps, but barrier-free access is available at Bexhill Road and Old Poplar Row. To reach Old Poplar Row, travel south on Meadow-wood Drive to Bob-o-link Road. Turn left on Bob-o-link Road and left onto Old Poplar Row. Bexhill Road runs south from Lakeshore Road West in Clarkson. Limited street parking is available at each of these entrances.

Wheelchair and Stroller Accessible

Birdwatching

Photography

Wildlife Viewing

Dogs on Leash Allowed

No Bicycles Allowed

It was 6:30 on a frost-bitten fall morning when I arrived at Rattray Marsh. In my rush to get there for the sunrise, I'd forgotten my gloves at home and it only took about three minutes for my ever-cold fingers to start tingling. I remember grumbling about the cold — and my forgetfulness — as I shoved my hands deep into my coat pockets for the stroll along Rattray's main boardwalk.

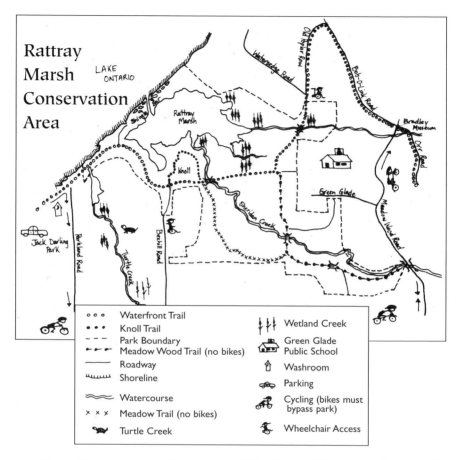

Rattray Marsh Conservation Area

LAKE ONTARIO

Rattray Marsh

Knoll

Jack Darling Park

Parkland Road

Turtle Creek

Bexhill Road

Sheridan Creek

Green Glade

Meadow Wood Road

Watersedge Road

Old Poplar Row

Bob-O-Link Road

Old Road

Bradley Museum

○ ○ ○	Waterfront Trail	⫼	Wetland Creek
● ● ●	Knoll Trail		Green Glade Public School
– – –	Park Boundary		
●–●–	Meadow Wood Trail (no bikes)	⬇	Washroom
―――	Roadway	🚗	Parking
ᨑᨑᨑ	Shoreline	🚲	Cycling (bikes must bypass park)
∿∿∿	Watercourse		
× × ×	Meadow Trail (no bikes)	♿	Wheelchair Access
🐢	Turtle Creek		

Now, I'm a very tactile person. It's almost like I need to touch something to be sure that it's actually there. That kind of approach usually works well in nature — with warm hands, that is. It's funny how hard it is to experience something when one of your primary sensory tools isn't available. One consolation — at least I wouldn't reach out and touch any poison ivy.

As I sat on a log on the beach side of Rattray's shinglebar wetland, I surveyed the scene around me. This remarkable nature reserve is located in the heart of a suburban area yet it's alive with the sights and sounds of a wild place. The first rays of an incredible pink and orange sunrise warmed my face; to my right, seven ring-billed gulls in search of a handout squawked their morning hellos.

Rattray's shinglebar wetland is the last of its kind between St. Catharines and Oshawa. The wave action of Lake Ontario deposits

Fall colours seem to last a lot longer at Rattray Marsh.

sediments and cobblestones across the mouth of the wetland, slowly forming a natural dam that stops the flow of water out into the lake. Once the water inside the marsh reaches a critical level, the dam is washed out, the water drains and the cycle repeats itself.

I closed my eyes and almost immediately the soothing sound of the lake's waves washed over me. The rhythmic flow of the water lulled me into an inner sense of calm and my mind wandered along a happy journey of past adventures. I could have sat there for hours, breathing in the cool smell of the water and reminiscing about so many incredible experiences, if a voice hadn't cracked the silence: "Jan... JAN! Turn around!"

Rose, my partner in this adventure, has taught me many things about the art of seeing, the greatest of which is to always look behind me. There, high overhead, were two brightly illuminated jetstreams that seemed to curl up and out of the park. I looked through the viewfinder of her camera and saw the scene you see here now. While I may have worked to eliminate those obviously human elements from my amateur compositions, Rose had framed them in a way that captured Rattray's uniqueness in a single scene: urban wild.

Surrounded on three sides by urban development, this 33-hectare lakefront sanctuary is home to an unbelievable 428 species of plants, 227 types of birds, 26 kinds of mammals, 18 varieties of reptiles and amphibians and 11 fish species. Birdwatchers flock to Rattray Marsh throughout the year to view migrating and breeding species, including: American bittern, green heron, wood duck, common yellowthroat, black tern, virginia rail, ruffed grouse, marsh wren, yellow warbler, sora, killdeer and more. I was treated to the thin *what-cheer cheer cheer cheer* of the brilliant northern cardinal and the familiar *dee-dee-dee* of the black-capped chickadee on my early morning walk. The white-tailed deer, beaver, red fox and rabbit who make their homes in the marsh were obviously too frightened by my teeth-chattering routine to emerge from their warm beds.

Now, I have to admit that I'm terrible at remembering plant names. Bird species come easily to me, often to the point where I can even recognize a bird the first time I see it, just from the description in my field guide. Plant names? Forget it. Most of the time, I just end up sounding silly when I describe things like the extraordinarily beautiful trout lily as that mottle-leafed plant with the droopy yellow flower.

Every hiker has seen a trout lily but, like me, may not have known its name. These delicate yellow flowers bloom only until June when the overhead tree foliage erupts to cut off their light supply. Remarkably, the trout lilies you see in Rattray Marsh and other locations may be up to 300 years old. The plant lives in colonies and sends out underground runners to produce new bulbs. Every spring, the new bulbs send up leaf shoots in search of light, but it will take at least five full years for the plant to flower, if it flowers at all. The process repeats itself year after year and decade after decade, forming an intricate network of roots that actually help to hold the soil together.

I sat down on the edge of the boardwalk where it crosses Sheridan Creek. I would have dipped my hand in the water (it's that tactile thing again) if the water level had been higher. This seemingly tiny creek originates in the middle of the city of Mississauga and funnels urban run-off into the marsh. Like Minesing Swamp, Rattray Marsh acts as a giant filter, removing pollutants and sediment from the water supply. Sitting there on the boardwalk, I realized that as great a cleansing system as a wetland is, there is simply no way it can filter out all of the paints, chemicals, fertilizers and toxins that are dumped into our storm sewers. Ultimately, the contaminants make their way to the lake — and our drinking water. Something has to give.

As hiking trails go, Rattray Marsh is one of the easiest trails mentioned in this book. The wide, elevated boardwalks are well maintained and make the pathway very stroller and wheelchair friendly. During my visit, I shared the path with fitness walkers, dog walkers and joggers, all of whom paused to share a warm hello with me. This place is cool, and next time, I'll bring some gloves.

There is No New Water

Like most other land-based plants and animals, humans need fresh water — the world's scarcest type of water — to survive. More than 99 per cent of the earth's water is salty, frozen in glaciers and ice sheets, or stored deep underground. Less than 1 percent of this vital life source is easy to access.

Canadians are among the lucky ones. We have 25 per cent of the world's fresh water but our thirst for water is phenomenal. Canadians use more water per person than any other people on the planet except Americans, and worldwide consumption is escalating.

Conservation Authorities monitor the quality of the water in our rivers, creeks and streams; help stop erosion; restore stream beds to their natural states; promote responsible water consumption and conservation; and more. This work helps ensure that the vital life sources we enjoy today will be available for the generations of tomorrow.

This butterfly meadow is bursting with activity every summer.

Snowy owls are occasional winter residents in this urban park.

Tommy Thompson Park

HIGHLIGHTS   Rivals Point Pelee as a birdwatcher's paradise. Lots of monarch butterflies. Close to 400 plant species makes the park a regular destination for amateur botanists. Smooth paved trail makes family visiting easy.

DIFFICULTY   Novice

TRAILS   Length: 5 km, one-way
MARKERS   None.
SURFACE   Main trail paved; side trails are footpaths.
TYPE   Linear

LINKS   Waterfront Trail

FACILITIES   Parking

OPEN   Weekends and holidays only, year round. (During winter, the park may close periodically due to unsafe conditions.)

OWNED AND OPERATED BY
The Toronto and Region Conservation Authority

DIRECTIONS   The park is located at the foot of Leslie Street in Toronto. Take the Don Valley Parkway south to Lakeshore Boulevard and travel east to Leslie Street. Turn right onto Leslie Street and go south to the parking area of the park. You can also take the TTC to the corner of Leslie and Commissioners Streets, and then walk south to the park.

Wheelchair and Stroller Accessible

Birdwatching

Butterfly Watching

Photography

Rollerblading

Cycling

No Dogs Allowed

"See you tomorrow at five," shouted Rose as she waved goodbye after work. I don't know why I ever agreed to get up before dawn on a Saturday morning to go on a wild goose — in this case, coyote — chase at Tommy Thompson Park. Have you ever tried to go to bed at eight o'clock on a Friday night? Thought not.

I arrived, bleary-eyed and bristly-tailed, at the base of Leslie Street on the stroke of five. Rose was her usual cheery morning self (have I mentioned yet that I'm pretty much nocturnal?) and her camera bag

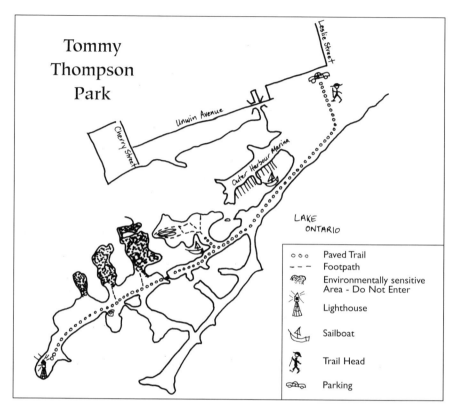

was packed and ready to go. I unloaded my trusty purple steed and we rode into the park as the sun began to rise. This had better be worth it.

Rose led the way through the gate, over the bridge and down the road toward the lighthouse. Suddenly, she raised her left arm to signal me to stop and I promptly braked beside her. "Over there," she whispered, "beside the pond. That's where the den is supposed to be." We quickly dismounted and rolled our bikes off the road. We tiptoed around the back of the pond and peered over the ridge. Sure enough, there was a mound of dirt near an old pipe. Maybe there were coyotes in this park after all.

Rose unzipped her bag as quietly as she could and unpacked her prize cameras. She was ready for anything. I, on the other hand, was cold and uncomfortable on my concrete throne. Tommy Thompson Park lies on the Leslie Street Spit, an outcropping of land that was artificially created using clean construction fill from locations across Toronto and materials dredged from the inner harbour. Concrete blocks, rebar (the metal rods inserted into concrete to give it even more strength) and other rubble expose the park's origins along the entire stretch of the spit.

As the sun began to climb higher in the sky, I began to wonder if the den might be empty. Coyotes are early risers and they should have been out by now. I started to squirm and Rose quickly shushed me to settle down. She wasn't about to miss her shot. Maybe the joke was on us. After all, the coyote is considered the trickster in First Nations folklore. It is supposed to teach us the balance of wisdom and folly. Right about then, I did feel like the wise fool. By ten o'clock, we gave up and set out on another wild goose chase — except this one did come true.

As we rode back to the park entrance, I spotted an interesting bird along the outer edge of the spit. We quickly hopped off our bikes and raised our binoculars to try a game of I-spy. We took turns pointing to different birds, trying to identify them. There were so many, we couldn't keep up. (Fingers can only work so fast when turning the pages of a dog-eared field guide.)

I had my nose in my guide when we both heard the strangest noise. It sounded like helicopter blades cutting the wind. When I looked up, I couldn't believe my eyes. Four whistling swans, with their distinctive black bills and two-metre wingspans, were coming in

This common snapping turtle was busy laying her eggs
beside the paved trail when this picture was snapped.

for a landing and we were in their flight path. I hit the deck with a thump and Rose dove for her camera bag. She missed the shot and I scraped my knee on a piece of rubble, but none of that mattered. Another bird story for the water cooler.

The brush with the swans shouldn't have surprised us. Close to 300 kinds of birds, including 45 breeding species, have been spotted in the park known as Toronto's Point Pelee. Five species of colonial waterbirds — ring-billed gulls, herring gulls, common terns, black-crowned night-herons and double-crested cormorants — nest here in significant numbers. The park is the first piece of land that migratory birds touch down on before and after a long lake crossing, so spring and fall bring warblers, sparrows, shorebirds and raptors by the hundreds. Not surprisingly, monarch butterflies also often use the park as a migratory staging area. When the thermometer drops, northern birds like snowy, saw-whet, boreal and long-eared owls move into the park in search of food.

Rose confirmed those stories — she had seen a snowy owl and a northern saw-whet in the park, and has the pictures to prove it. If she can find those kinds of birds, I'll meet her in the park at 5 A.M. any day.

Toronto's Point Pelee

Like Point Pelee, Tommy Thompson Park has been designated as an internationally recognized Important Bird Area (IBA). BirdLife International began the IBA program in Europe in 1985 in an effort to conserve and protect important habitat areas before bird species are put at risk. Since most bird species are migratory, other nations soon joined the program and there is now a global network of more than 100 IBA countries.

A site can be named an Important Bird Area in one of four categories: threatened species, restricted breeding ranges, biome (e.g. Tundra or Great Plains) restricted species or bird concentrations. Tommy Thompson Park received its Important Bird Area designation in the bird concentration category. Huge numbers of ring-billed gulls and black crowned night herons nest in the park. In fact, somewhere around 6% of the world's nesting population of ring-billed gulls can be found at Tommy Thompson Park.

CENTRAL

Fresh-baked bread — pass the butter.

Black Creek Pioneer Village

HIGHLIGHTS   One of Toronto's leading family-friendly attractions. Major events held in every season, including a fantastic Victorian Christmas. A gardener's paradise. Farm animals, historical crafts and people in old-fashioned costumes make history fun.

DIFFICULTY   Novice

TRAILS   Length: Unknown
MARKERS   Street signs
SURFACE   Boardwalks and dirt roads
TYPE   Looped

FACILITIES   Parking, washrooms, pay telephones, restaurant, gift shops, information desk.

OPEN   Daily, May 1 to December 31, except Christmas Day.

OWNED AND OPERATED BY
The Toronto and Region Conservation Authority

DIRECTIONS   From Highway 400, travel north to the Steeles Avenue exit. From the light, turn left (you'll be travelling east along Steeles Avenue). The first major street you will come to is Jane Street. Travel through the intersection and move immediately to the right hand lane. Turn right at Murray Ross Parkway and drive south to the Village entrance.

R aspberries are my favourite berry. As young teens, my brother and I used to compete for the best berry patch on our farm. He was in charge of the strawberries and I controlled the raspberries. We'd work diligently (at least that's how I remember it) to cull the weeds, nurture the new shoots and harvest the berries so our mom could make her delicious jams and pies. When I saw the gardener at Black Creek Pioneer Village gathering raspberries, my mouth began to water with the memories of freshly made desserts. I'd give my left arm (okay, not literally) for a mouthful of a homemade pie.

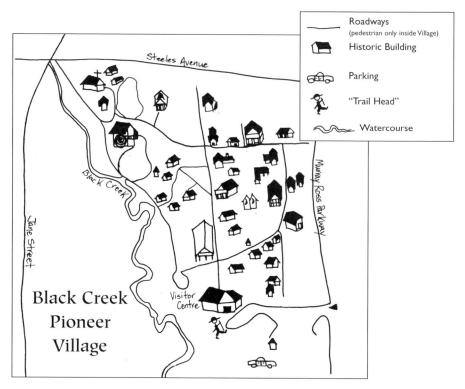

Black Creek Pioneer Village is unlike any other park in this book. It doesn't have any forests or cliffs, and you can't fish or mountain bike or even cross-country ski there. So why is it in this book? Let me tell you. Black Creek is an adventure like no other I'd ever experienced before — it's an adventure in time.

When I stepped onto the Black Creek boardwalk for the very first time, it was like stepping into a time warp — back to the 1860s. All of a sudden, everything around me felt as if it had slowed down. The driver of a horse-drawn wagon waved as he passed by. A beautiful woman in a four-foot-wide dress and a bonnet said hello when I met her on the street. And the clang of the blacksmith's iron rang through the air. I have to admit that I'd never gone on a hike quite like this before.

Black Creek Pioneer Village is one of the premiere family attractions in Toronto and it's owned and operated by — surprise — its local Conservation Authority (now you see the connection). Toronto and Region Conservation purchased the land on which the Village

Roblin's Mill.

now stands in the late 1950s and slowly turned it into a fully-functioning historical attraction. Since it opened in the 1960s, Black Creek has been visited by more than eight and a half million people — yes, that number is correct — from all around the world. I have to say I felt privileged to be one of them.

The gardener disappeared into the huge white inn at the end of the boardwalk. (I had to follow him — he had my raspberries.) My guide map said it was the Half Way House (the half way point on a long journey, not a pioneer parole centre) so I opened the door and went in. Rooms filled with antique furniture greeted me from both sides, and a giant staircase opened up in front of me. But it was the smell of wood smoke and home baking that pulled me to the back of the building, and it was there that I found my raspberries.

The kitchen table was covered with freshly baked bread — 34 loaves to be exact. The baker had just pulled them from her huge brick bake-oven (yes, she had baked them all at once) and she was ready to bake her next creations — oatmeal cookies and apple-raspberry

These gentle giants are almost 2 metres tall — at their shoulders!

cobbler. I was in seventh heaven. While I was waiting for the delicious treats to bake, she told me some of her baking secrets. Her flour was ground in the mill right there in the Village. I knew where the raspberries came from but her apple story was incredible. In the middle of the Village's sheep pasture stand six 180-year-old apple trees. (They sure bring a whole new meaning to old-growth trees.) The apples in the pies had been picked from those trees the previous fall and dried in the old-fashioned way for use in her desserts.

Her stories about life in the 19th century made the time pass quickly and before I knew it, the cobbler was ready. I paid for my piece, thanked her for her stories and went outside to savour my treat. I sat down on the peaceful verandah of the local store and watched the world go by between bites. That cobbler was almost as good as my mom's pie.

My hike around the village took me from building to building and garden to garden. I bumped into the gardener, who told me that almost every flower and vegetable he planted was a kind that would have been found in Canada some 140 years ago (and some of his rose varieties date back all the way to the 16th-century). I stopped by the sheep pasture to take a look at those apple trees, and some inquisitive lambs stopped by for a visit. I hopped on that horse-drawn taxi I mentioned earlier and took a spin around town. And I visited the mill, the tin shop and a whole bunch of old houses. The people are so friendly here — what a great place to bring kids.

As I left the village after that first visit, I thought about my high school history experience that I told you about earlier in the book. That episode had made me overlook Black Creek Pioneer Village for so many years. But I wasn't about to make that mistake again. Not with fresh bread, oatmeal cookies and apple-raspberry cobbler on the line.

19th-Century Herbs

Medicinal herbs were a staple of all 19th-century gardens, including those found at Black Creek Pioneer Village. Roses were so important to early health care that they were among the first things planted. Various rose lotions, teas, syrups and conserves were used to treat everything from inflamed eyelids and sore throats to migraine headaches, constipation and ulcers.

Garlic was used to treat colds, coughs, asthma and bronchitis, and was even given to croupy hens. Feverfew was the 19th-century aspirin and, when taken with rum, it was particularly good for toothaches.

Many plants, including dill, caraway, cardamom and fennel, had medicinal uses and were used to flavour food. Resin-scented sweet fern, bitter tansy and wild mint were excellent natural pest deterrents and may have been used to deal with fleas, ticks, mites, ants and even bedbugs.

Beautiful wildflowers line the banks of the Holland River.

A 55mm macro lens was used
to capture this green frog's grin.

Rogers Reservoir Conservation Area

Birdwatching

Cycling

Dogs on Leash Allowed

HIGHLIGHTS   Peaceful marsh. Bird viewing platform. A natural oasis in the midst of a rapidly urbanizing area.

DIFFICULTY   Novice

TRAILS   Length: 4.2 km in total (West Bank Trail, 2 km; East Bank Trail, 2.2 km)

MARKERS   None, follows Holland River

SURFACE TYPE   Footpath and compacted, screened gravel
Linear

FACILITIES   Parking

OPEN   Year-round access, dawn to dusk

OWNED AND OPERATED BY
Lake Simcoe Region Conservation Authority

DIRECTIONS   Follow Davis Drive/Highway 9 into Newmarket to Main Street North. Travel north approximately 2 km. Access to park is available from Green Lane and Main Street.

My mother always told me that I should never judge a book by its cover. Her words rang in my ears the day I visited Rogers Reservoir. The park looked like so many other Conservation Areas in the province — quiet, unassuming and maybe even a little ordinary. Then I heard my mother's voice and I knew I'd better listen.

I slowly got out of my car and trekked off to the bird viewing tower at the north end of the reservoir. I plunked my behind down on the tower, swung my feet over the edge and rested my elbows on the middle rail. I'm going to let them come to me, I thought. And boy, did they come.

My mom also said patience is a virtue, but I wasn't feeling the least bit virtuous that morning. My mood broke when I tuned into the loud chattering and whistling of a gridiron filled with red-winged blackbirds. It seemed like they were everywhere around me with

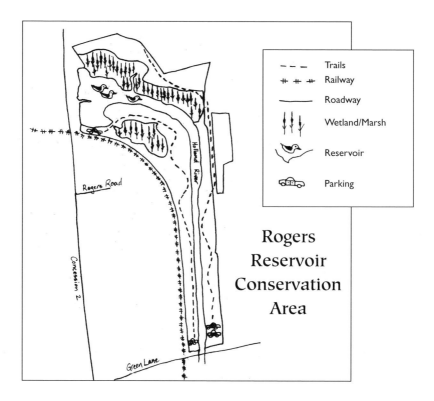

Rogers
Reservoir
Conservation
Area

voices ranging from the single-noted *check* to the slurred, sports-whistle-like *konk-la-reee*. It was almost like watching a circus. Each male would sing loudly until another male came too close for comfort, and then the chase would be on. Those crazy birds spent what seemed like hours jealously protecting their tiny pieces of wetland real estate from would-be invaders. Their intensity made me smile. After all, isn't passion what life's all about?

Well, sometimes single-minded passion isn't such a great thing. There was an odd, musky smell in the air that I couldn't quite pinpoint and the birds obviously didn't notice it either. There was a flourish at the edge of the cattails and suddenly one of the tenors was gone. I turned my head just in time to see a cute, arch-backed brown creature steal away with the bird in its jaws. That cute little critter was none other than a mink, one of Ontario's smallest and most savage killers.

Mink are pretty single-minded, too. They have been known to scamper right over the feet of stationary human spectators in search of a meal. I actually experienced almost the exact phenomenon when I was a kid. I was out for a dirt bike ride near the creek on my family's farm when something came at me and struck my left leg. I slammed on the brakes thinking that I had just hit some poor animal, but when I got the bike back to the spot of the impact, I found a beady-eyed little mink with its jaws wrapped around the neck of a tiny rabbit. It had been so focused on capturing its prey that it hadn't even heard the sound of an approaching motorcycle. And no matter how much yelling or engine revving I did then, the mink just looked at me. That brush with the feisty mink made me glad I was now on the viewing platform.

I waited a while and then struck off up the trail for the other end of the reservoir. Along the way, I passed a great blue heron, a gaggle of Canada geese and a variety of sandpipers, none of which I could immediately identify. I also heard the unique whinny of a sora, a secretive little marsh bird that is more often heard than seen. As I sat in my car after my 4-km round-trip hike, I thought of my mom and what she had said, and I realized that her words conveyed a wisdom that I should pay closer attention to. But isn't that the case with all moms?

How to Buy Binoculars

1. Ask other birders what they use and request a test-drive of their models. You'll gain experience in testing different models and you'll receive great insights from practical use.

2. Search out a store that specializes both in binoculars and in birding.

3. Define your needs before you shop. Are you a backyard birder or a hawk watcher? Is weight a concern? Do you canoe? Wear glasses?

3. Know your price point and express your needs clearly to the salesperson.

5. Don't be intimidated — the ultimate judge is you. Test-drive each pair of binoculars using the same criteria: ease of use, personal comfort and feel, ease of focus, brightness, close focus, magnification, field of view and colour of image. Don't put too much emphasis on magnification — anything between 7x and 10x is fine for most people.

*The buckets were hung on the trees with care,
in the hope that syrup soon would be there.*

The sugar shack lies idle for most of the year.

Sheppard's Bush Conservation Area

Maple Syrup

Birdwatching

Dogs on Leash Allowed

HIGHLIGHTS: Awesome maple syrup program in spring. Fitness trail. Great Fall colours.

DIFFICULTY: Novice

TRAILS	Length: Varying lengths
MARKERS	None
SURFACE	Footpath
TYPE	Looped

FACILITIES Parking, picnic tables

OPEN Year-round access, dawn to dusk

OWNED AND OPERATED BY
Lake Simcoe Region Conservation Authority

DIRECTIONS The main entrance is off Industry Street in the Town of Aurora. A second entrance is available from Industrial Parkway.

W hen I was a child, I thought that tapping the trees during maple syrup season actually hurt them. Ahhhh, the imagination of a child.... All right, all right, I admit it. I believed that silly story right up until I visited Maplefest at Sheppard's Bush Conservation Area.

The friendly staff at Maplefest set me straight. A tap in a tree is just like a small cut for a human and in no way does it stop or slow down the tree's growth. In fact, the amount of sap taken each season is only a fraction of the total amount of sap inside the tree. To minimize potential damage, a tree needs to be about 80 cm in diameter at an average chest level (about 40 years old) before it can be tapped, and the number of taps on each tree is limited to one for every 20 cm of tree diameter. New holes are drilled each year so that the tree can heal the old holes itself. I felt a whole lot better after I heard that.

For me, the best part of syrup season is the samples. Every year, I try the sap first. This clear liquid that comes straight from the tree

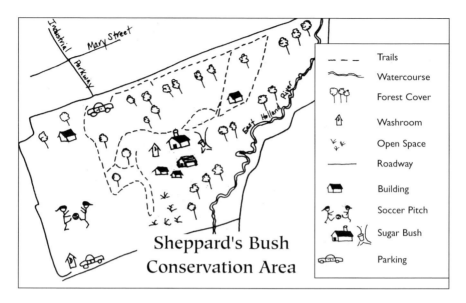

doesn't look like much but it does have a vaguely sweet taste. Then comes the deliciously sweet, slightly smoky maple syrup. My mouth waters every time I think about it.

Maple sap contains about 2 – 4% dissolved sugar and is boiled (and boiled and boiled and...) to make the syrup. I know that doesn't mean much but this might — it takes about 40 litres of sap to make 1 litre of maple syrup. I saw the process first hand at Sheppard's Bush and all I can say is that it takes a mighty patient person to make this liquid gold. Good things come to those who wait, I guess.

The art of making maple syrup is really a science. The sap flow from the trees is entirely dependent on the right weather conditions. Days must be warm (4 to 8 degrees Celsius) and nights must be below freezing (-5 to -10 degrees Celsius). If the weather gets cold and stays cold, the sap will stop flowing. If the weather gets warm and buds appear on the trees, the sap turns bitter and syrup season is done. If that isn't enough, the finished syrup must have a sugar density of exactly 66.5% — no more and no less — to be considered the real thing.

I never knew maple syrup making was so darn complex. And to think my brother and I used to make it on the wood stove when we were kids. We only ever produced enough syrup to smother four heaping bowls of vanilla ice cream. Hmmm... I think I'd better check to see if I have any maple syrup left in the fridge.

The best fall colours can be found in a sugar bush.

Layer for Winter Warmth

You've heard it so many times, but how do you actually do it?

THE FIRST LAYER of clothes wicks the perspiration away from your skin so you can stay dry. Synthetic materials are often the best at wicking and surprisingly, cotton is the worst. One of the best ways to keep your fingers and toes warm is to add a wicking layer, or liner, to your mitts and socks.

THE MID-LAYER is your primary insulating layer and one of the most critical components of your system. Depending on the weather conditions and your exercise level, this layer can range from nothing at all to heavy goose down. Cross-country skiers and winter runners often wear no mid-layer, while families out for a leisurely walk would probably choose a much thicker mid-layer.

THE OUTER LAYER acts as a barrier to the elements. It should block the wind, keep snow and rain from getting in, and let perspiration out! What a big job! Choose your outer layer carefully. It should be light, functional for lots of activities — and waterproof if you can afford it.

At the top of the famous "99 Steps"
with a view to the Oak Ridges Moraine.

Thornton Bales Conservation Area

Birdwatching

Photography

Snowshoeing

Horseback Riding

Dogs on Leash Allowed

HIGHLIGHTS   The "99 Steps" beautiful birch grove lines the trail head. Well known as a place to see red-shouldered hawks. Located on the Oak Ridges Moraine.

DIFFICULTY   Intermediate

TRAILS   Length: 2 km
MARKERS   None
SURFACE   Footpath and steps
TYPE   Looped, with two short linear trails at the east side of the area.

FACILITIES   Parking, picnic area

OPEN   Year-round access, dawn to dusk

OWNED AND OPERATED BY
Lake Simcoe Region Conservation Authority

DIRECTIONS   Access is off Mulock Sideroad, 3 km west of Highway 11 (Yonge Street), in Newmarket.

I recognized the scream instantly. It was as haunting as the first time I'd ever heard it. *Kee-yer, kee-yer.* I put my fingers behind my ears and cupped them forward to amplify the sound. Where was it coming from?

Thornton Bales is well known to birders as a place to find the elusive red-shouldered hawk, and I was determined that I was going to spot myself a hawk. As I quietly walked in the direction of the sound, I looked high into the trees. There are very few red-shouldered hawks left in the Toronto region and they are rarely spotted. This was going to be difficult.

These beautiful birds live in large blocks of mature, dense deciduous forests and feed on amphibians, reptiles and rodents from nearby wetlands. Sadly, they have not adapted well to the rapid clearing of forests in Canada's most heavily populated area and now

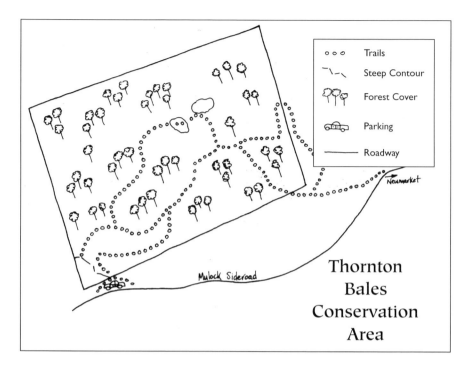

Trails

Steep Contour

Forest Cover

Parking

Roadway

Neumarket

Mulock Sideroad

Thornton
Bales
Conservation
Area

breed only in the remnants of native forest along the Oak Ridges Moraine.

I crouched down to wait for another scream. I knew I was in the general vicinity of the bird but I hadn't yet spotted it. After what seemed like an eternity, but was really only about five or six minutes, I heard the scream again coming from well ahead and to my left. I followed the sound for as far as I could but the ground cover and fallen logs soon stopped me in my tracks. I scanned my binoculars up across the canopy of trees in the hope that I might catch a glimpse of this magnificent bird. No luck.

By this point, I was pretty discouraged. And the initial enthusiasm that had carried me down Thornton Bales' notorious "99 Steps" was just about gone. My body slumped with the thought of the 54-metre climb back up to where I had parked my car.

I sat down on a fallen tree and yanked out my water bottle. Of course, in my frustration the top slipped open and I squirted water across my shirt. So, maybe it wasn't my day. After a few minutes of thought — and some time to dry off — I decided to change my perspective on my day. After all, I did hear a red-shouldered hawk, which is a lot more than most people can say. Maybe this day was about sounds and not sights, so I lay back on the log, closed my eyes and opened my ears. Am I ever glad I did.

I often think that people who live or work in the city turn their ears down. Who wouldn't, with all the incessant noise that accompanies "civilization"? It takes a concentrated effort to open your ears to the sounds of nature when you've spent a lifetime trying to hide from the noises around you. As I lay back on the log, I tried to tune in to the natural rhythms around me. Believe me, it was not easy. The closest parallel I can draw to the opening of my ears is the art of meditation (which I'm miserable at). Every little sound distracts me and I just can't focus enough to meditate. I was determined that this would be different.

I became so in tune with the quietness around me that I almost fell off that log when a sound like a machine gun shook the forest around me. Startled, I opened my eyes to remind myself I wasn't in the line

The elusive red-shouldered hawk hides deep in the forest. Can you see it? (Here's a hint — follow the fork in the tree wayyyyy up…)

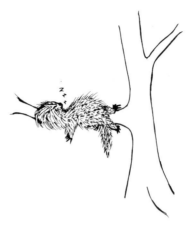

Trees — Dead or Alive?

Trees have four lives: the young tree, the mature tree, the dead standing tree and the fallen tree. Each life is as essential as the others.

The first life as a seedling and young tree is a struggle for survival. The young tree fights with hundreds of other seedlings for light and nourishment. If it is successful, the tree will move into its second life — maturity.

Mature trees continue to grow, perhaps even reaching their maximum size in the forest. Those trees that do not fall victim to a chainsaw often die of natural causes courtesy of lightning strikes, insect invasion, disease, fire or flooding.

Death is inevitable but that doesn't mean the tree's life is over. Dead standing trees provide homes for eagles and insects, and food for woodpeckers and bats.

The fourth and last life of a tree starts when it falls. Dead trees can last almost 100 years on the forest floor, providing nourishment for new seedlings and habitat for plants and animals.

Fallen trees provide critical nourishment and habitat for seedlings, amphibians and other creatures.

of the crossfire. The sound became clearer and I soon realized that it was the powerful drumming of a pileated woodpecker. As tempted as I was to jump up to follow the sound, I resisted the urge. Pileateds rarely afford anyone an audience so I simply sat and enjoyed its powerful tree whacking.

The sights of nature can be incredibly powerful, but so can the sounds if you let them wash over you. Suddenly, the climb back up those "99 Steps" seemed a lot less ominous. This was a day — and a place — to remember.

From high atop the Vista Trail.

Rouge Park

Birdwatching

Wildlife Viewing

Fishing

Cross-country Skiing

Snowshoeing

Photography

Campground

Dogs on Leash Allowed

HIGHLIGHTS   Largest urban park in North America (bigger than Central Park). Loads of birds and wildlife. Fantastic trout and salmon fishing. A wild place accessible by TTC. Right beside the Toronto Zoo.

DIFFICULTY   Multiple levels

TRAILS   Length: 8 km in total (Riverside Trail, 3km; Vista Trail, including loop, 2.2 km; Orchard Trail, 1.6 km; Loop north of Beare Landfill Access Road to Meadowvale Road, 1.3 km).

MARKERS   White signs with green and blue directional arrows

SURFACE   Footpath

TYPE   Linear, with small loop at north end.

FACILITIES   Parking, picnic areas

OPEN   Year-round access, dawn to dusk.

OPERATED BY The Toronto and Region Conservation Authority

DIRECTIONS   Exit Highway 401 at Sheppard Ave. East and head north. Turn east on Kingston Road/Highway 2 and look for the Glen Rouge Campground sign. You can access the southern tip of the trails from there.

YOU CAN ALSO PARK AT PEARSE HOUSE, the trail's northern access point, just east of the main entrance to the Toronto Zoo. Exit Highway 401 at Meadowvale Road and head north, following the car access signs to the Zoo. At the light, turn right and Pearse House will be on your right. Parking is also available on Twyn Rivers Drive and on Old Finch Avenue west of the Toronto Zoo. There is also a large parking lot on Twyn Rivers Drive.

FOR TTC ACCESS to Rouge Park, call (416) 393-INFO.

I've always wanted to visit New York's Central Park. It's a vibrant and active — and dangerous — place to be. And it used to be North America's largest urban park until the late 1990s when the Greater Toronto Area's own Rouge Park quietly moved into first place on that list.

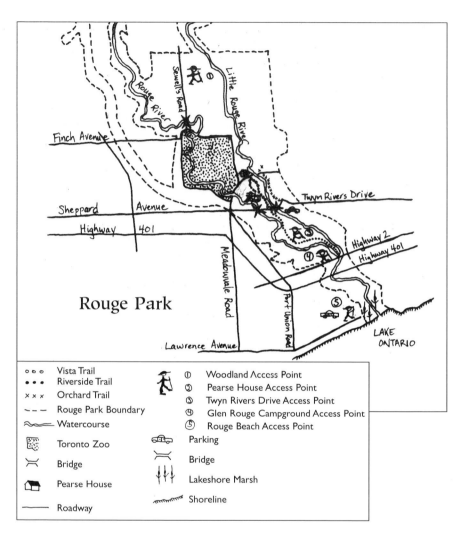

The Rouge is a totally different park from its Manhattan-based sister. Instead of paved paths, the Rouge has dirt footpaths. Instead of mown grass, it has wild meadows. Instead of stone statues, it has old-growth forest. And instead of the fancy restaurant in the Central Park Boathouse, the Rouge has... well, nothing. The Rouge is exactly the way Ontarians want it — rugged and undeveloped. And the Greater Toronto Area is the better for it.

I've been to the Rouge dozens of times but one particular visit stands out. It was fall and the overnight temperature had dipped below zero. The sun was still hidden by the horizon when I stepped

The author and a friend explore the Rouge valley on snowshoes.

out of my car and I could see my breath in the crisp morning air. Luckily, I'd remembered my gloves (there would be no replay of my frozen finger debacle at Rattray Marsh).

I parked beside the bridge on Twyn Rivers Drive so I could watch the salmon run (a term used to described the fall spawn). I learned the true meaning of perseverance from those fish. There they were, so close that I could probably have touched their backs if I had stretched out my arms. They were struggling through water that was so shallow in places that it didn't even cover their gills. They were exhausted from the effort and their sides were scarred from their journey, but these incredible fish were focused on only one thing — to find a way upstream to spawn.

I watched in horror as a friend's dog plunged into the river for a swim, oblivious to the fish and their purpose. The dog stepped on one of the extraordinary creatures, fatally wounding the tired fish. (I knew there was a good reason for leash laws.) But before that salmon died, it mustered all its remaining strength and slapped that dog across the snout with its tail. Delicious irony, don't you think?

I turned my attention away from the river for a minute and saw something that I'd never paid close attention to before. Plain and simple frost. It was everywhere. It rimmed the edges of tree leaves and lined the delicate stems of dried weeds and wildflowers. It glistened in the early morning light with a freshness I had never seen before. I paused and shook my head at all the years I'd overlooked the beauty of nature's smallest things. What a shame.

It was there, in that first meadow along the Riverside Trail, that I saw my first coyote. I think it was as surprised to see me as I was to see it. We both froze for a split second, and then the wild dog that looked a lot like a bushy grey German shepherd trotted off with its head and its tail down. Coyotes are extremely adaptive creatures and can successfully co-exist with humans — except we barely even notice. They move around us virtually undetected so it's rare to actually see one. You're much more likely to hear their high-pitched howling. And we think we go to look at nature. Have you ever stopped to think that it's more likely that nature is looking at us?

The well-camouflaged trickster is more often heard than seen.

Coyotes aren't big game hunters like their wolf cousins. Instead, they are fairly opportunistic and will eat whatever they can catch. This might include rabbits, birds and even fish, and they are known to eat fruit, seeds and other vegetarian fare. I have to admit a surge of fear swept over me when I first saw it but that soon passed. They aren't even interested in humans. (We can be so vain sometimes.)

Early morning and dusk are the best times to see wildlife, and my sightings weren't finished yet. On my way back to my car, I rounded a corner to see a large buck and two does drinking from the cool, clear waters of the Rouge River. They saw me before I could stop and they quickly turned and waved goodbye with their white tails. White-tailed deer must be one of the most stressed-out animals anywhere. They are constantly watching for predators, they eat on the run and they bounce around nervously like tightly coiled springs. Wait a minute. Maybe that's not unlike Central Park — or even corporate Canada.

How to See Wildlife — Lesson 2

Now that you've mastered the art of slowing down and tuning in, it's time to graduate to the next level — the fox walk. Have you ever watched a fox walk? Foxes are confident, energetic walkers that have a real spring in their steps. When you examine their walk closely, you'll find it's the healthiest and quietest way to get around in the woods.

Hold your body upright and face the horizon. Do not lean forward or look at the ground — let your feet become your eyes. Take short, easy steps, placing each foot down gently almost in front of the other. Instead of walking heel first, land on the outside of your foot and roll to the inside before moving your weight forward. And instead of pushing off with your calves, lift your feet with your thighs.

No, the fox walk is not easy but it is healthy. It makes your feet strong, straightens your back, gives you stability and allows you to walk much more quietly. Keep practising and if it helps, imagine you have a bowling ball between your knees. You'll soon be an expert.

Thistles are a favourite food of the American goldfinch.

Bruce's Mill Conservation Area

Swimming

Birdwatching

Butterfly Watching

Wildlife Viewing

Photography

Maple Syrup

Cross-country Skiing

Snowshoeing

Driving Range

Dogs on Leash Allowed

HIGHLIGHTS   Sugarbush Maple Syrup Festival. Bacteria-free swimming hole, complete with sandy beach (unsupervised). Beautiful butterfly meadow. Golf academy located on site.

DIFFICULTY   Intermediate

TRAILS   Length: 5 trails, 12.5 km total length.
MARKERS   Colour-coded
SURFACE   Compacted screened gravel, footpath and mowed meadow.
TYPE   Looped

FACILITIES   Children's playground, washrooms, baseball diamond.

OPEN   WINTER: late February to early April for maple syrup, 10 A.M. to 4 P.M.; SUMMER: end of April to Thanksgiving, 9 A.M. to dusk. Pedestrian traffic only, during off-season.

OWNED AND OPERATED BY
The Toronto and Region Conservation Authority

DIRECTIONS   Exit Highway 404 north at Stouffville Road. Travel 3 km east on Stouffville Road to the park entrance.

I can remember the day as if it was yesterday. I must have been ten, maybe eleven, and my little brother came in the house yelling about a cloud of butterflies. I, being almost two years his senior, promptly corrected him with my fifth grade science skills — clouds are filled with water droplets or ice crystals, I told him, and not butterflies.

He insisted I was wrong and promptly dragged me, my mom, my dad and our dog outside to the apple trees. "There!" he said, "Clouds!" And sure enough, thousands and thousands of monarch butterflies were descending en masse — and looking a lot like clouds — onto our

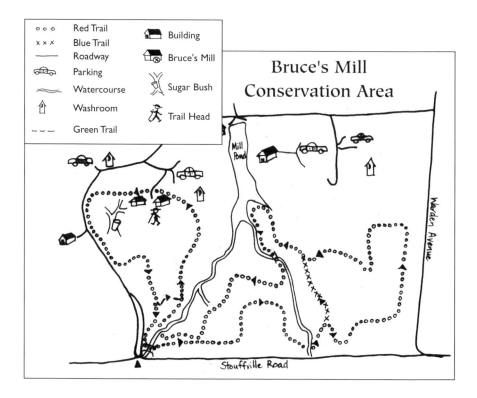

apple trees. I thought of those monarch clouds the day I wandered into the butterfly meadow at Bruce's Mill.

It was a sunny, warm day and the local butterflies were particularly busy. Monarchs fluttered from flower to flower, and at least two dozen beautiful yellow tiger swallowtails danced in the sunbeams. As you well know, I'm no expert when it comes to identifying plants. I was only able to recognize a few of the more common flowers, such as purple coneflower and black-eyed susan. (I think it's high time I invested in a field guide on plants.)

Butterflies are fascinating bugs. Swallowtails first taste the nectar of flowers with taste buds on their feet and if it passes the taste test, they greedily slurp up the nectar while frantically fluttering their wings. Monarchs are the snowbirds of the butterfly world, migrating to Mexico each fall to avoid the chill of winter. In August and September, they gorge themselves on nectar, gather by the thousands on hilltops and fields, and catch a ride south the same way hawks do — on thermals.

Red-spotted purple butterflies adore milkweed.

Bruce's Mill is a park with a lot of extremes. Across the road from the butterfly garden, I found a golf driving range. Up the creek from the beach, I discovered an osprey nest. And only a few hundred metres from a busy picnic shelter, I spotted a white-tailed deer as it bounded across the path. There almost seems to be a natural ebb and flow — a harmonious balance between human presence and nature — at the park. I couldn't help but smile.

I also made a wintertime trek to Bruce's Mill for the Sugarbush Maple Syrup Festival. I'm convinced maple syrup is a comfort food — or at least the annual pilgrimage to the sugar bush is a comfort ritual. There's an incredible calm that sweeps over you as you enter the woods. The snow crunched under foot as I made my way through the trees. A wood fire crackled and steam gently rose from a giant cast-iron kettle. The sweet smell of liquid gold filled my nostrils.

The Festival is Bruce's Mill's biggest event and they really pull out all the stops. Horse-drawn wagons transport young and old deep into the sugar bush. Fiddle music fills the air. Friendly staff dressed in lumberjack outfits lead tours along the sugar trail. And the delicious smells of wood smoke and syrup tempt even the strongest-willed dieters to feast on a stack of steaming hot pancakes with sausages. I watched in amazement as a friend's two-and-a-half-year-old devoured five plate-sized pancakes in one sitting (without the benefit of a single utensil). Now that's the way to eat!

The success of the spring syrup season is entirely dependent on the amount of sunlight captured by the leaves of the sugar maples. Warm and sunny fall days accelerate the production of sugars in the leaves. Once the temperature dips below seven degrees Celsius, the sugars become trapped in the leaves by a waterproof layer that forms at the end of stems. Chlorophyll production then stops and the leaves turn red from the accumulation of sugar. The more sugar in the leaves, the redder they become — and the more sap there is the following spring.

So, come September, keep your eyes peeled for vivid red maple leaves and clouds of monarch butterflies. And start planning your spring and summer excursions to Bruce's Mill.

All aboard the maple syrup train!

Old Habits Die Hard

We are creatures of habit. We want to protect the biodiversity around us without really changing the way we consume things. Perhaps our current crisis is not with the environment...maybe it's with our own behaviour.

The Conservation Foundation and Conservation Authorities across Ontario are passionately committed to helping us change the way we view the world around us. They have created highly acclaimed educational programs and projects that promote good environmental citizenship among individuals, schools and private companies.

Over the years, Ontario's Conservation Authorities have introduced powerful conservation messages and practices to millions of school-age children and general public. Clearly, there is some hope.

Along the boardwalk...

Kortright Centre for Conservation

HIGHLIGHTS   Daily hikes, special events and evening programs offered by on-staff naturalists. Home to the Sugarbush Maple Syrup Festival. Close to 200 species of birds have been recorded on-site. Home to two million honey bees.

DIFFICULTY   Multiple Levels

TRAILS   Length: 15.6 km (Power Trip Trail, 1 km; Maple Sugar Bush Trail, 1.4 km; Cold Creek and Wetland Trail, 1.2 km; Forestry Path, 2 km; two, 5 km trails along the edges of open fields in the southern and northeast portions of the park).

MARKERS   None. Trails well defined.

SURFACE   Mostly compacted screened gravel with some boardwalk. Sensitive slope is paved.

TYPE   Looped

LINKS   McMichael Canadian Art Collection Trail

OPEN   10 A.M. to 4 P.M. daily except Christmas Day.

SPECIAL   Kortright is a public demonstration site for alternative energies and sustainable technologies.

FACILITIES   Parking, washrooms, cafeteria, interpretive centre, gift shop.

OWNED AND OPERATED BY
The Toronto and Region Conservation Authority

DIRECTIONS   From Highway 400 north, exit at Major Mackenzie Drive. Travel west for approximately three kilometres to Pine Valley Drive. Turn left and the Kortright gate will be on the right side of the road. Well signed.

Interpretive Centre

Cross-country Skiing

Maple Syrup

Birdwatching

Wildlife Viewing

Photography

Cafeteria

Dogs on Leash Allowed

I felt kind of silly. There I stood, boots and socks safely up on the trail with one foot in one creek and the other in another. The naturalist who was with me excitedly proclaimed, "I can feel the difference. Can you feel the difference?" I had to pinch myself to make sure I wasn't dreaming. Nope, I was on a stream safari at the Kortright Centre, standing with one bare foot in Cold Creek and the other in the East Humber River. And believe it or not, there was a difference.

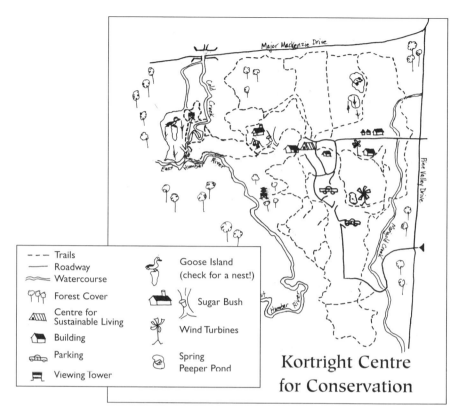

Kortright Centre for Conservation

Legend:
- - - Trails
—— Roadway
~~ Watercourse
Forest Cover
Centre for Sustainable Living
Building
Parking
Viewing Tower
Goose Island (check for a nest!)
Sugar Bush
Wind Turbines
Spring Peeper Pond

It was August (otherwise you wouldn't catch me near a major river without my trusty lifejacket) and I had embarked on an adventure along the trails at Kortright. Yes, there was a difference between the two waterways — Cold Creek definitely lived up to its name, even on this hot summer day. The two waterways were so close together but so very different. I soon found out that the creek is colder because it runs through a shaded valley; the river is warmer because it flows through open farmland where the sun can warm the water. And since warm water holds less oxygen than cold water, fish like brook trout that thrive in the creek cannot survive in the Humber.

The entire Kortright experience is different — in a really great way. This was the first park where I went on a hike led by a professional. Depending on the time of year, staff naturalists lead hikes to the honey house, along the power trail, through the sugar bush, along the board walks and all the way to the birdfeeder trail. So much information and so little time.

Kortright naturalists are master storytellers who captivate their audiences by transforming even the tiniest detail of nature into a remarkable yarn. And the stories they tell embed themselves in your mind. Take, for instance, the squirrel tale. According to my naturalist guide, the forests that rose after the last glaciers had retreated were so dense that squirrels could have hopped all the way from Windsor to Montreal without ever touching the ground. Probably an exaggeration, but I got the point (and I've remembered that story for more than a year and a half).

My real passion is birds so after my tour I grabbed one of Kortright's birdwatching brochures and struck out on my own. Close to 200 species, including more than 25 different warblers, have been recorded at the Centre and I was determined to see as many as I could. As I made my way down the steep path behind the main Kortright building, my ears were filled with the songs of a number of familiar birds. But when I got to the edge of the of meadow below the sugar bush, an unfamiliar sound rang out.

The high-pitched song seemed particularly urgent. Once I closed my eyes, I was able to identify the strange tune (*sweet-sweet, chew-chew*) and follow the general direction of the enthusiastic soloist. There, in a

The great horned owl's ears
are hidden on the sides of its head — not in those fluffy horns.

The praying mantis blends in easily with its leafy surroundings.

treetop along the edge of the meadow, sat a brilliant blue indigo bunting. Now, indigo buntings are actually black but their feathers (males only) refract light to produce the beautiful blue colour. And while they love to sing, indigo buntings won't make the avian Top 100 any time soon. (They reminded me of the tone-deaf alto in the church choir from my youth.)

I chose to turn back and go into the sugar bush. It was strange to see the sugar shack surrounded by green leaves. I passed the building and went north toward the hedgerows. I was deep in thought when I flushed three, crow-sized pileated woodpeckers out of their hiding spot along the edge of the trail. I think they startled me as much as I startled them. They cackled an angry *wicka-wicka* as they flew away and by the time I had recovered enough to realize what had happened, all I saw were three bright red heads in the distance. Pileateds mate for life, so I must have stumbled upon a mother, father and offspring. It's a picture I won't soon forget.

The sun started to sink toward the horizon and I reluctantly retreated to my car. Next time, I won't spend so much time standing in a creek. I think I'll try an owl prowl or a bat night or maybe even catch a dogsled race. There's so much to learn about nature — and Kortright is a great place to do it.

Drumroll, please...

It's showtime whenever a wood-pecker is around. Woodpeckers are loud and flashy, and hard to mistake for any other bird. They pound on hollow trees, create a fantastic racket by drumming on metal roofs — usually at the crack of dawn — and their repertoire of completely unmusical whoops, rattles and cackles can carry for close to a third of a kilometre.

Woodpeckers are the only birds with skulls thick enough to get away with banging their head against hard objects. Thick bones coupled with extra-strong head muscles and cushioning tissues inside the skull protect the bird's brain when it chisels into trees.

Even if you don't hear or see a woodpecker, you may find evidence of drill holes in the trees. Downy woodpeckers excavate small round holes, hairy woodpeckers create oblong holes and the unmistakable pileateds strip-mine huge rectangular holes 7-10 cm wide. Next time you're out hiking, look for the unmistakable evidence of a woodpecker's handiwork — wood chips at the base of a tree.

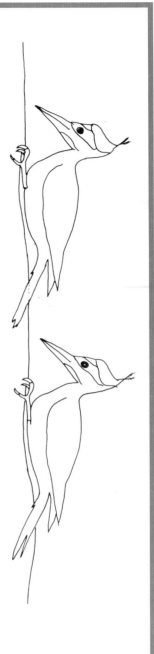

Tamaracks are the only coniferous trees that change colour in fall.

Whitchurch Conservation Area

HIGHLIGHTS   Trails connect to York Region Forest trail system. Heavily forested with a pond.

DIFFICULTY   Novice

TRAILS   Length: Unknown
MARKERS   None
SURFACE   Forest path
TYPE   Linear and looped

FACILITIES   Parking, picnic facilities, washrooms

OPEN   Year-round access, dawn to dusk

OWNED AND OPERATED BY
Lake Simcoe Region Conservation Authority

DIRECTIONS   Travel 10 km east along the Aurora Sideroad (Regional Road 15) from the Town of Aurora. The parking lot is on the south side of the road.

I stumbled onto Whitchurch quite by accident. I had been driving in circles in search of another park when I finally pulled off the Aurora Road to check my directions one last time. My frustration was mounting and I was just about to give up my search when I noticed the partially hidden Whitchurch sign just ahead of me. It was then that I heard my wise mother's words, "When life gives you lemons, make lemonade." Whitchurch was about to become my lemonade.

The thrill of adventure sometimes comes from the unknown. I had no guide to the trails, no idea about how big (or small) the park was, or any sense of what I might find there, but I embraced the challenge and set off with my camera gear. "Live a little," I say.

I crested the first little hill and the space opened up to a small pond. The water level was down at least 20 to 30 cm and the water lay

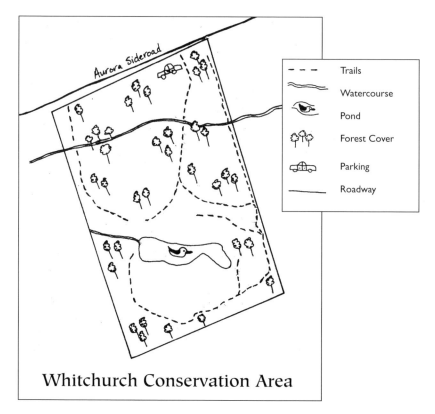

- - -	Trails
∿∿	Watercourse
👁	Pond
🌳🌳	Forest Cover
🚗	Parking
———	Roadway

Aurora Sideroad

Whitchurch Conservation Area

still in the centre of the depression. You don't really think about the effects of a long, dry summer until they hit you square in the face. When life gives you lemons... As I stepped up to the edge of the water, a handful of frogs splashed into the water from the comfort of their sunny slumbering spots. The bank was lined with them. Greens, leopards... you name it, they were there. I took one step to my right and more frogs splashed away. Another step and then another and still another, until what seemed like a chorus line of frogs dove away into the pond. I playfully circled the pond to incite a circuitous splash — it reminded me of that movie where one by one, swimmers dove into a pool in a spectacle of synchronicity. I laughed out loud at the thought.

Play. It's a remarkable thing. It's too bad we lose the ability as we "mature." I skipped away from the side of the pond with an open mind and an open heart. It felt great to be carefree — until I tripped over a tree root and tumbled heavily to the ground. When life gives you... I had to laugh at myself because there was no one else there to

The air always seems fresher deep inside a forest.

Green frogs are common in most wetlands.

do it. Well, that's not entirely true. I heard a bird scream in what I was sure was laughter and I quickly took to my feet to find my mocking audience.

As the trail tracked along a white board fence, I saw my avian comedian land in a huge maple tree. It was a red-shouldered hawk, the raptor that had eluded me at Thornton Bales, and I realized that this impressive bird wasn't there to mock me. It was almost as if the hawk's presence was a sign just for me. North America's First Peoples believe strongly in the spiritual and magical powers of all creatures, and the hawk totem is particularly powerful. The appearance of a hawk is supposed to awaken one's vision and stimulate hope and new ideas. When life gives you lemons, make lemonade.

The hawk took flight and I raced after it along the path. Before I knew it, I was in the middle of an estate subdivision, far from the heart of the park, and my hawk was gone. It seems the subdivision lies directly between the park and the York Regional Forest's maze of trails. Whitchurch may be small but it's clearly a very important link in a much larger natural chain. I'm glad I made some lemonade that day because there was sure a lot more there than first met my eye.

Spirit Totems

A totem is any natural object, animal or being that you feel closely associated with during your lifetime. To discover your totem, think about which animal or bird has always fascinated you or what creature you have seen most frequently when you have been outside. You should also consider which animal, if any, you are afraid of or have had dreams about. These are your totems.

Totems are incredibly powerful symbols that demonstrate the deep reverence and respect our country's First Peoples have for nature and her creatures. Wouldn't it be nice if we all gave her that same respect? Here are a few totems and some suggestions of their possible meanings. Is your totem in this list?

Chickadees = cheerful and truthful expression

Coyotes = wisdom and folly

Deer = gentleness and innocence

Eagles = illumination of spirit, healing and creation

Hawks = visionary power and guardianship

Hummingbirds = tireless joy

Mice = attention to detail

Nuthatches = higher wisdom

Spiders = creativity

Waxwings = gentleness and courtesy

Whales = creation and power of song

Burnt marshmallows are a camping tradition.

Albion Hills Conservation Area

HIGHLIGHTS   Recreation paradise — summer and winter.
27 km of groomed and track-set cross-country ski trails.
Bacteria-free swimming in the Albion Hills lake.
Lots of campsites for those who want to rough it close to home.

DIFFICULTY   Multiple Levels

TRAILS   Length: 27 km (Red Trail, 9 km; Green Trail,
2 km; Blue Trail, 6 km; Yellow Trail, 2.5 km; Black Loop, 7 km),
plus new mountain bike trails under development for 2000.

MARKERS   Colour-coded marks on trees.
SURFACE   Footpaths
TYPE   Looped

LINKS   Bruce Trail
Caledon Trailway
Trans Canada Trail
Humber Valley Heritage Trail

FACILITIES   Parking, picnic areas, washrooms, boat
rentals, pay telephones, campground (serviced and unserviced
sites), ski equipment rentals, campground store, snack bar.

OPEN   Seasonal. Last Saturday in April to Thanksgiving, 9 A.M. to
dusk. Open December to March for cross-country skiing as snow conditions
permit. Pedestrian traffic only, at all other times.

OWNED AND OPERATED BY
The Toronto and Region Conservation Authority

DIRECTIONS   On Highway 400, travel north to Highway 9. Travel west on
Highway 9 to Highway 50. Turn left and travel south on Highway 50 through
Palgrave to the park entrance.

Swimming

Cycling

Birdwatching

Wildlife Viewing

Fishing

Photography

Canoeing

Cross-country Skiing

Snowshoeing

Tobogganing

Ice Skating

Campground

Snack Bar

Dogs on Leash Allowed

T here's something about kids and snow. They seem to be made for
each other. I can remember my childhood when the first flakes
of the white stuff meant a wild sprint to find my snow pants.
And what was the first thing my brother and I would do after a good

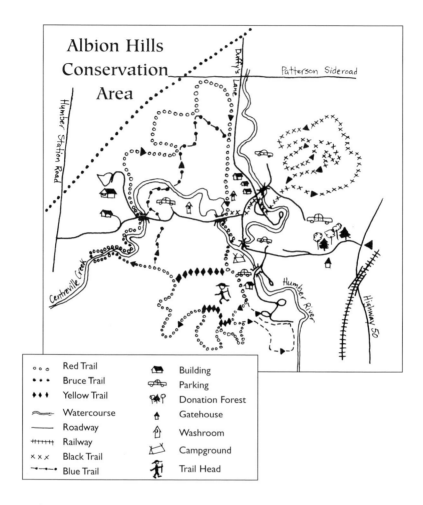

snowball fight? We'd head for the nearest hill and slide until it was dark. (Who could forget those bright blue crazy carpets?) The little kid in me came out again the day I heard Albion Hills had a toboggan hill. I was there — bad back and all.

I borrowed a neighbour's big wooden toboggan and hit the slopes. That first run down the hill was just as good as I remembered it — the snow washed up into my face, the wind whipped by my partially covered ears, and my fingers began to tingle with the realization that I'd brought the wrong gloves for this sport. It was at the bottom of the run that I realized why thirty-somethings shouldn't catapult down a snow-covered slope on their behinds. It was a long climb back up to the top of the hill. (I had somehow forgotten that rather critical part.

There are trails for cross-country skiers of all abilities.

Isn't that what tow-lifts were invented for?) After three long hikes up the hill, I gave up the struggle. I needed to warm up and Albion's heated chalet was calling my name.

Fortified by a boost of hot chocolate, I decided to test my luck on the cross-country ski trails. It had been a good 15 years since I had learned to ski in gym class but I was ready for the challenge. I rented some boots and a pair of blue and white skis and I was off — sort of. Skiing isn't exactly like riding a bike. (Let's just say I was glad I was wearing waterproof pants). I only lost my balance twice — before the first turn, that is — but I was unfazed — I knew I could do it.

Now, I'm certainly no Bjorn Daehle but things picked up pretty soon. I told myself that it was important to practise my kick, so I let all the little kids pass me on the way up the first hill. Then I remembered my favourite part of skiing — the hills. The trail forked and I took the left leg (the one with the hill). I put my skis in the tracks and crouched into a tuck. Okay, the hill was more like a bump but it was lots of fun. I'm glad I went left, hill or no hill. This was the green trail (nice and short) and it connected to the yellow trail (for a grand total of 4.5 km). My legs were already tired and the long trails

An immature broad-winged hawk peers down from its perch.

were just too daunting. I decided to save the long ones for summer mountain biking.

Mountain biking at Albion is lots of fun, too (at least I don't fall quite so often). The trails are old fire roads so they're nice and wide — perfect for riding with friends. I even took some time after my ride to cool off with a splash in the lake. (Don't worry, it was shallow so I was safe.) And if my back would have tolerated a dirt mattress, I would have pitched my tent in the Albion campground. There's nothing like sleeping under the stars — as long as there's some decent padding underneath.

Albion is a naturalist's playground, too. The extensive forest systems inside the park are home to a diverse mix of species, including red-shouldered and broad-winged hawks, black-throated blue and black-throated green warblers (yes, there's a big difference — look for the black throated blues in the mixed forest and the black-throated greens in the conifers), wild turkeys, porcupines, mink, beaver and white-tailed deer. I caught sight of about eight or nine wild turkeys along one of the trails, but by the time I stopped my bike, they had all taken to the air. Out of naivety, I didn't think they could fly — they can but they sure won't receive any awards for grace.

The turkeys are the only wild creatures I've seen at Albion, but that doesn't mean much. I've turned Albion into my own little playground and with so many things to do, I really can't expect to see any wild things around me. I spend way too much time shouting and laughing to just blend into the trees.

Winter Photo Tricks

❄ **Underexposed images?** Snow reflects a lot of light that can easily fool your camera's light meter. To compensate for this brightness, fill your frame with something grey (a large rock works really well), take an exposure reading and re-frame your original shot using the f-stop and shutter speed determined by the rock. You can also fill your frame with the back of your hand and take a reading from that!

❄ **Brrrr....** Cold weather can zap your camera, your batteries and you! Keep your camera cold and your battery warm (your pocket will do). Always keep an extra battery in your bag — if the cold drains your battery, you may miss the image you waited all day for.

❄ **Emotion.** Falling snow stirs many emotions and memories. If you want to capture falling snow as streaks across your image, use a long shutter speed like 1/30 or 1/15. (A tripod is essential when you use long shutter speeds.)

*Find that kid deep inside — dangle your feet off the dock
and skip a few stones at the setting sun.*

Scanlon Creek Conservation Area

HIGHLIGHTS	Soft, sandy beach.
	Glacial erratics pepper the landscape.
	Great fall-colour destination.
DIFFICULTY	Intermediate
TRAILS	Length: 4.6 km (Kingfisher Trail, 3.2 km; Maple Trail, 1.4 km).
MARKERS	Blue Kingfisher signs, red maple signs
SURFACE	Footpaths, some boardwalk
TYPE	Looped
FACILITIES	Sandy beach, washrooms
OPEN	Year-round access

OWNED AND OPERATED BY
Lake Simcoe Region Conservation Authority

DIRECTIONS   Travel north on Simcoe County Road 4 (formerly Highway 11/Yonge Street) from Bradford and follow signs that direct traffic to the main gate on Concession Road 9, just east of Simcoe County Road 4.

Cycling

Swimming

Fishing

Birdwatching

Wildlife Viewing

Photography

Cross-country Skiing

Snowshoeing

Dogs on Leash Allowed

One of the most valuable lessons I've learned from nature took place at Scanlon Creek. I'd somehow injured my lower back a few days before my visit and ever so stubbornly, I insisted on keeping to my schedule. Anyone with low back pain knows how hard it is to walk on flat terrain but there I was at Scanlon Creek, ready to tackle the trails. My normal gait is best described as a step below sprint so you can imagine how frustrated I must have been. Remarkably, that's were the magic stepped in.

I was forced to slow down my pace to less than a quarter of my normal speed and despite the pain, I'm glad I took my time. Once I got over feeling sorry for myself, I started to see things that I hadn't seen in a long, long time. All around me, black-capped chickadees were

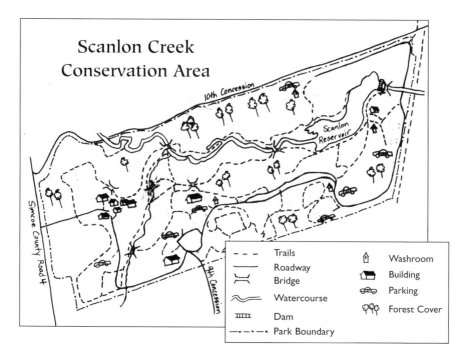

joyfully singing and playing acrobatically in the trees. The wind sang a gentle song through the mixed forest and the wide, leaf-lined roadway reminded me of the canopied gravel road that our family always took to reach my favourite aunt and uncle's farm.

I read somewhere that the biggest tragedy humanity experiences is not the suffering we endure but all of the things we miss along our way. Think about it for a second. We race from place to place, appointment to appointment, without even considering all of the things that are happening around us. And when we actually get out in nature, how many of us hike so fast that we never see the birds, the trees and the wildlife around us? I've done it and I'll bet you have, too. "Stop the world! I want to get off!"

With my bad back, I rediscovered the cardinal rule of nature appreciation — slow down! As I made my way along the path, my senses seemed to come alive. The earthy smell of the humus that lines the forest floor filled my nostrils. I suddenly became aware of the gentle rustling of mice and other rodents under the leaf cover, and out of the corner of my eye, I caught sight of a red squirrel leaping from treetop to treetop. I paused to run my fingers over the bark of a

Freedom on a two-wheeler.

decaying tree trunk and around the frayed edges of a woodpecker's excavation. This was living.

The ground was covered with wildflowers, including the bright red columbine. The columbine's tubular blooms hang upside down and its bright colour captures the eye of the hummingbird, one of our most delightful summer visitors. The deep wing-buzz of the ruby-throated hummingbird is often heard long before the tiny bird is ever seen. Once visible, these tiny birds are often mistaken for large dragonflies. Their frantic wing beating is driven by a phenomenal metabolism, and these nectar-loving birds must refill their tiny bellies every 10 minutes or so. I scanned the bed of flowers for one of these colourful visitors but at that moment, none were to be seen.

I continued (slowly) along the trail past the picnic shelters to the small lake in the northeast corner of the area. The edge of the lake is sprinkled with odd-looking boulders and rocks called erratics that were pushed into the area by glaciers. The last great Ice Age, which occurred some 15,000–20,000 years ago, pushed a wall of ice across Ontario and parts of north-central United States. As the ice retreated northward, a number of meltwater lakes formed, including Lakes Algonquin and Iroquois. Evidence of this period of great turmoil can be found at Scanlon Creek. Part of a beach formed by Lake Algonquin exists as a scarp (just a funny name for a steep slope or cliff) in the central part of the park.

I sat down on the boardwalk that separates the lake and a large marshy area, and waited for the life to come to me. It was also a good excuse to rest my weary back. After a few minutes, I noticed a beautiful painted turtle sunning itself on a floating log and heard the distinctive call of the tiny marsh wren. The turtle reminded me of the Ojibway creation legend that says our earth was created when an industrious muskrat brought mud from the bottom of the waters and placed it on a turtle's back. Muskrats spend most of their time in the water and can even lower their metabolism enough to stay under water for well over 10 minutes. I searched the waters of the marsh for this giant swimming mouse but none were close to the turtle that day.

As I made my way back to my car, I was passed by a friendly mountain biker. At that point, I would have given anything for a two-wheeled reprieve for my back. Then again, I wouldn't have enjoyed

Late summer wetland flowers crowd the boardwalk.

my surroundings nearly as much on a speeding bicycle. I'd save the cycling for another day. Scanlon Creek is one of the few parks described in this book that has mountain biking trails and I know I'll take advantage of them sometime soon. My top priority right then was to head home to a nice Epsom salts bath and a good book. My new guide to animal tracking would certainly fit the bill.

As I mentioned at the beginning of this story, I learned a very valuable lesson that day at Scanlon Creek. I'll try not to let the important details slip right by me again. Missing out on life really is a greater suffering than a bad back.

Signs of Life

Nature enthusiasts often look for paw or hoof prints in the mud or snow to help them track wildlife. And while these signs are helpful for those in the know, most of us would probably have trouble differentiating the tracks of a domestic dog from those of a wild coyote. Animal highways and other signs are often easier — and more visible — to the untrained eye.

Look around. You'll likely see trails of matted vegetation that lead to watering holes or feeding and bedding areas. Sometimes the ground may even be worn down into a U-shape by frequent use.

Beds are relatively easy to identify. Look for depressions of well-matted vegetation that conform to the body shape of an animal. Beds sometimes contain large amounts of hair or leaves.

Some animals leaves rubs on nearby trees or soil. An animal that is large enough to go over a fallen log may rub the bark off with its belly; a small animal may rub the bottom bark off with its back. Broken twigs, clumps of hair on branches and scat are also good ways to identify the presence of wildlife.

The beautiful Humber River meanders through the park.

Boyd Conservation Area

Birdwatching

Wildlife Viewing

Photography

Dogs on Leash Allowed

HIGHLIGHTS	A wildlife and bird refuge in the forest beyond the river. 17 well-groomed picnic areas.
DIFFICULTY	Novice
TRAILS	Length: Unknown
MARKERS	Not applicable
SURFACE	Footpath
TYPE	Linear
FACILITIES	Washrooms, two bocce courts, basketball court
OPEN	Summer: end of April to Thanksgiving, 9 A.M. to dusk Pedestrian traffic only, during off-season.

OWNED AND OPERATED BY
The Toronto and Region Conservation Authority

DIRECTIONS   Travel north on Highway 400 to Rutherford Road. Travel west along Rutherford Road to Islington Avenue. Turn left onto Islington Avenue and travel approximately 1 km to the park entrance.

N ever judge a book by its cover." My mother's wisdom rang in my ears again. It felt like déja vu. So many central Ontario Conservation Areas look so ordinary. But like Rogers Reservoir, Boyd was full of magic — just as my mother's wisdom predicted.

In the woods behind Boyd's precisely manicured picnic areas and busy bocce courts lies a treasure trove of wild things. Plants, mammals, birds — their presence seems like a miracle given the pressures of development around the park. The trees are home to scarlet tanagers, black-and-white and blackburnian warblers, grey tree frogs and more. Spring beauties, trilliums, wild leek and hepatica

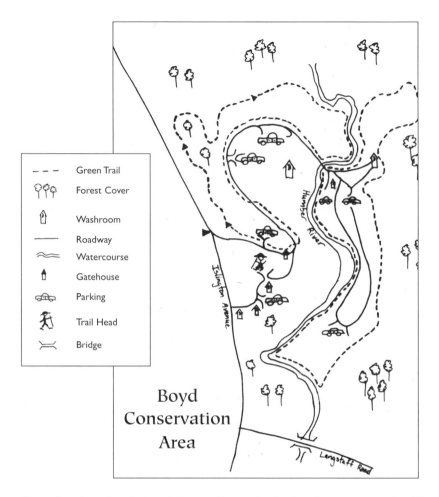

Boyd
Conservation
Area

Legend:
- - - Green Trail
🌳 Forest Cover
⌂ Washroom
— Roadway
≈ Watercourse
⌂ Gatehouse
🚗 Parking
🚶 Trail Head
⋈ Bridge

line the river banks and forest floor. And, thanks to some significant conservation work to remove downstream barriers, salmon and trout will soon share the river with the resident beavers and their friends.

The beaver dam at Boyd is the work of one of nature's most remarkable engineers. Its construction reminded me of the abandoned dam in Enniskillen, but with one major difference. A heavy spring storm had indeed swept the dam apart in the centre, opening the structure like two heavy gates. The industrious engineers had quickly reconstructed the dam but left the offending doors protruding from the new structure. I could only stand in wonder of the remarkable resilience — and intelligence — of nature. (But then again, weren't the most incredible human systems first perfected by the natural world?)

The jack-in-the-pulpit is a common spring flower in the Boyd forest.

My first visit to Boyd came on a rainy late-April afternoon and I soon discovered that spring is one of the best times to visit this unassuming place. The forest floor was carpeted with white trilliums and jack-in-the-pulpits — easy flowers for a non-plant person to identify. Both flowers appear after the early blooming hepatica and spring beauties have disappeared.

The white trillium is Ontario's floral emblem. It takes about seven years from the time a trillium seed sprouts until it produces its first flower. Its three-petalled blooms survive a mere two to three weeks, so enjoy them while they last (just don't pick them). The jack-in-the-pulpit's green flower lasts a little longer but it still takes seven long years to show its face. Like with the trillium, you must resist the temptation to pick these beautiful flowers — jack-in-the-pulpits are toxic and even a small amount of sap on bare skin will likely cause irritation. (Keep the antihistamines handy.)

As the sun began to set, I started back to my car. It was then that I heard the strangest noise. It sounded like distant sleigh bells. I stopped in my tracks and listened. The sound of the distant bells began to swell and soon I was surrounded by a loud chorus of shrill voices. Suddenly it hit me — spring peepers. They emerge by the

A grey tree frog uses its tiny suction-cup fingers to cling to this branch.

Don't pick the trilliums —
they take seven long years to bloom

hundreds on rainy evenings like this and squeal to their heart's content. Spring peepers are barely an inch long but their 120-decibel call rivals the loudness of an airport runway. This was no church choir but it was still a remarkable sound. I was smitten. Bullfrogs at Terra Cotta, green frogs at Whitchurch and now spring peepers at Boyd — the more amphibians, the better.

Inspired by my peeper serenade, I returned to Boyd in late May. My mission this time? Grey tree frogs, the chimpanzees of the frog world. These slightly larger (maximum two inches) nocturnal chameleons live high in the treetops and inflate their throats like balloons to emit a loud, deep trill. Although these frogs are somewhat quieter than their thunderous peeper buddies, the sound is no less impressive.

If you're fortunate enough to see a tree frog, you'll be amazed by its incredible ability to blend into its surroundings. It can change from bright green to brown and then grey in as little as a half hour. I was lucky. I spotted one in mid-change and I gently lifted it from its perch on a leaf. It wrapped its sticky fingers around mine and before I knew it, it had leapt off to the nearest tree trunk. If I wasn't already infatuated with frogs, this experience would have done it.

As I left the park that day, I remembered my mother and her words. I resolved right then and there to call her to tell her she was right — and to apologize for all the teenage years that I didn't believe her.

Healthy Frogs, Healthy Humans

How can you tell if the environment is healthy for humans? Easy! Keep an eye on your friendly neighbourhood frogs and amphibians. Like the canary in the coal mine, these and other bellwether species can sound the first alarm to alert us to unstable and unhealthy local environments.

Frogs and amphibians have highly-permeable skin and are extremely sensitive to toxins, unhealthy water, habitat loss and other environmental upsets. Conservation Authorities are working to monitor a number of amphibian and mammal species to help us understand the current state of our local environments. Some of the results are alarming. Bullfrogs, pickerel frogs, spring peepers and grey treefrogs no longer live in the Toronto area south of Highway 7 and are all now listed as species of concern. There are currently no Eastern Newts, the tiny red amphibians that need both forests and wetlands to survive, in Toronto and the surrounding suburban areas.

Assistance from the public is needed to help monitor the changes in amphibian populations. Please contact your local Conservation Authority to find out how you can help.